YOU ARE Outrageously Blessed

RAE SIMONS

YOU ARE *Outrageously Blessed*

Inspiring Devotions for Women

BARBOUR
PUBLISHING

Print ISBN 979-8-89151-210-8

Text previously published as *God Calls You Blessed.*

Published by Barbour Publishing, Inc., 1810 Barbour Drive, Uhrichsville, Ohio 44683, www.barbourbooks.com

Our mission is to inspire the world with the life-changing message of the Bible.

Member of the Evangelical Christian Publishers Association

Printed in China.

And God blessed them. . . .

Genesis 1:22 KJV

In the very first chapter of the first book of the Bible, we read that God was already in the business of blessing. He created the world—and then He blessed it and its inhabitants. As you read through the Bible, chapter after chapter you'll find stories about God blessing His people, and you'll encounter promise after promise of blessing.

But what are we talking about when we use that familiar word *blessing*? Did you ever stop to think what it means to be blessed?

Merriam-Webster's Dictionary gives six definitions for *bless*:

1. to make sacred
2. to ask for God's help
3. to speak words of approval
4. to give happiness and health
5. to protect and preserve
6. to endow with a gift

God blesses you in all these ways. You are set aside to be God's holy dwelling place. Through Christ, you have the right to ask God for help and care. He speaks to you and affirms your identity; He gives you happiness and health; He protects you; and He gives you countless gifts!

And the best blessing of all is Jesus Himself. As Galatians 3:13–14 (MSG) says, "This is what happened when Jesus was nailed to the cross: He became a curse, and at the same time dissolved the curse. And now, because of that, the air is cleared. . . . We are all able to receive God's life, his Spirit, in and with us by believing." Through Jesus, you are richly and eternally blessed with the gift of life.

GOOD AND PERFECT GIFTS

Every good and perfect gift is from above, coming down from the Father of the heavenly lights, who does not change like shifting shadows.

JAMES 1:17 NIV

You are blessed because God has chosen to shower gifts on you.

These gifts are everywhere we turn, but sometimes we miss out on seeing them. We forget to notice simple things, like the warmth of the sun or the brilliant light that fills the sky at the end of the day. We may be so preoccupied with our worries and our busyness that we don't notice the smile on a child's face or the love in our spouse's embrace. We also may overlook God's even greater gifts, like His daily grace and the everyday gift of love He gives to us through His Spirit. But nevertheless, no matter how self-absorbed or dull-eyed we may be, God keeps pouring out His good and perfect gifts.

Lord, open my eyes to see Your many gifts.

THE BLESSING CIRCLE

"Give, and you will receive. Your gift will return to you in full—pressed down, shaken together to make room for more, running over, and poured into your lap. The amount you give will determine the amount you get back."

LUKE 6:38 NLT

Sometimes, we may close our hearts to God's blessings. How do we do that? With selfishness. With laziness. With our preoccupations and worries that keep us focused on our own selves.

But God longs to bless you. And the more you give to others—the more you turn away from your own self-centered interests and focus on others—the more room you will have in your life for God's blessings. The more you give away, the more God will give to you. The more you bless others with your love, your attention, your compassion, and your generosity, the more you will be blessed. It's the opposite of a vicious circle—a circle of blessing that never stops turning.

Show me, dear Lord, where I have shut myself off from Your blessings. Teach me to notice others and find ways to give of myself to them. Melt my selfishness, and give me a heart that overflows with love.

PEACE OF MIND

"Do not fear, for I am with you; do not be afraid,
for I am your God. I will strengthen you, I will also help you,
I will also uphold you with My righteous right hand."

ISAIAH 41:10 NASB

We all crave freedom from anxiety. We long for that quiet sense that all is as it should be—and yet everywhere we turn we see things that are clearly *not* as they should be. Sometimes, it seems as though fear and anxiety are just the natural state of affairs. We walk around with a tightness in our chests; we lie awake fretting over the future; we wake up dreading the day ahead. To ask for relief seems impossible, like too much to ask of God. After all, everyone has their share of troubles, and the world is full of strife. That's just reality.

But that's not the reality God wants you to experience. He wants to change your fear into confidence in Him. He longs for you to trust Him enough to give Him all your anxieties. And when you do, He will hold you up. You will be blessed with strength and peace of mind.

God, You know all the anxieties that fill my mind. I want to give them to You. Help me depend on You to make me strong.

YOUR NEEDS

My God will meet all your needs according to the riches of his glory in Christ Jesus.

PHILIPPIANS 4:19 NIV

God doesn't promise to fulfill every wish that enters your head—but He does say that He'll supply *all* your needs. He won't overlook any of them. Do you need a friend? Ask God to bring one into your life. Do you need help with your finances? Take it to God in prayer; you probably won't become suddenly wealthy, but God will help you find the answers you need. Do you need help making a decision? God will give you guidance. Maybe you need something as small and simple as time alone—or as big and complicated as help with a difficult family situation. Whatever it is, God can and will help. His resources are unlimited. You are blessed because God will take care of you.

God, You know my needs. Thank You that Your riches are infinite.

THROUGH JESUS

We all live off his generous abundance, gift after gift after gift. We got the basics from Moses, and then this exuberant giving and receiving, this endless knowing and understanding—all this came through Jesus, the Messiah.

JOHN 1:16–17 MSG

God is not stingy. He gives you gift after gift after gift, one after another, grace upon grace. Your entire life springs from His immense generosity. If you ever had the idea that following Jesus meant a narrow, restricted life, a life of saying no to pleasure, get that idea out of your head! As you follow Jesus, you enter into a joyful cycle of giving and receiving, with God at the center. Jesus came to share God's exuberance and gladness with you. You are blessed with wisdom, grace, and joy. Your very life springs from the blessing of Jesus, the Messiah.

Jesus, thank You for all You make possible in my life. Teach me to follow You more closely. I want to learn from You.

SPIRITUAL BLESSINGS

Blessed be the God and Father of our Lord Jesus Christ, who has blessed us with every spiritual blessing in the heavenly places in Christ.

EPHESIANS 1:3 NASB

This is an amazing verse. It's telling you that right now, spiritually speaking, you already possess all that God has to give to you. You may have to wait for these blessings to become visible in this world, but they are already yours. You don't have to wait to receive them until you die and go to heaven. And you don't have to earn them first; you don't have to work hard to become a "better" person. All these blessings already belong to you. They have your name written on them.

Thank You, heavenly Father, for gifting me with so many blessings. I can't wait to open them all!

WAYWARD THOUGHTS

The mind governed by the Spirit is life and peace.

ROMANS 8:6 NIV

All through the Bible, again and again God promises us peace. And yet our lives and our hearts are all too often shaken by conflicts and fears. How can we access the peace that God promises us? How can we experience it as something more than an all-too-fleeting emotion, a feeling that's almost impossible to hold on to?

In this verse, the apostle Paul gave us the answer: We need to allow our minds to be governed by the Holy Spirit. In another verse, Paul called it "taking every thought captive" (2 Corinthians 10:5 NASB). No one says this is easy. It takes self-discipline and practice to give our wayward thoughts to the Spirit.

You too can be blessed with life and peace. But you need to do your part. It's well worth the effort!

Spirit, I surrender to You all my thoughts. Take control of them. Help me make a habit of doing this until it becomes second nature.

YOUR CLOTHES

"And why worry about your clothing? Look at the lilies of the field and how they grow. They don't work or make their clothing, yet Solomon in all his glory was not dressed as beautifully as they are. And if God cares so wonderfully for wildflowers that are here today and thrown into the fire tomorrow, he will certainly care for you. Why do you have so little faith?"

MATTHEW 6:28–30 NLT

Do you ever worry about your clothes? Maybe you don't have the right thing to wear for a special event. Or maybe you can't afford to update your wardrobe, and you're starting to feel embarrassed wearing the same old things. God doesn't promise to make you into a fashion plate, but He does say that there is nothing too small or unimportant to bring to Him. Be like a flower, Jesus said in this passage of scripture, confident that God will provide you with all you need to reflect your inner beauty. Trust God to provide the clothing you need. He is waiting to bless you in so many ways—including through the clothes you wear!

God, I bring my wardrobe concerns to You.
Thank You that You care about anything that concerns me.

YOUR MONEY

"Bring the whole tithe into the storehouse, that there may be food in my house. Test me in this," says the LORD Almighty, "and see if I will not throw open the floodgates of heaven and pour out so much blessing that there will not be room enough to store it."

MALACHI 3:10 NIV

A tithe is considered to be 10 percent of a person's income. It's a rough guideline for how we are to share our resources with God—but we don't need to look at it as though it were a hard-and-fast number like a sales tax. The larger message behind the Bible's talk of tithing is that we are to share everything we have with God, including our money.

And the more you share with Him, the more He will bless you. "Test Me," the Lord says. "Try Me and see if I won't keep My word to you." This doesn't mean that if you give away all your money, God will transform you into a millionaire. The blessings you receive may not even be financial. But you can be confident that the more you give to God, the more richly you will be blessed.

Lord, give me a generous heart. Show me where I can contribute to Your kingdom here on earth. I want to give freely from the resources You have given me.

GREATER THAN YOU THINK

Now all glory to God, who is able, through his mighty power at work within us, to accomplish infinitely more than we might ask or think.

EPHESIANS 3:20 NLT

God may not answer prayer in exactly the way you hoped—but eventually, you will be able to see that His way was even better than anything you could have imagined. Your thoughts and imagination have limits, but God's mind is boundless, and His power is infinite. He is longing to bless you in ways you've never pictured. Don't hold Him back. Let Him give to you all that He can. The sky is the limit!

Dear Lord, sometimes I'm afraid to ask You for something. I don't want to be disappointed if You say no. Increase my confidence in Your love. Help me be assured that You will give me far more than I have ever thought. Your imagination is so much greater than mine!

A GENEROUS HEART

Now I say this: the one who sows sparingly will also reap sparingly, and the one who sows generously will also reap generously. Each one must do just as he has decided in his heart, not reluctantly or under compulsion, for God loves a cheerful giver.

2 CORINTHIANS 9:6–7 NASB

Again and again throughout the Bible, we read how important it is to give of our own resources to others. This could mean being generous with our money, or it could mean we give our time, happily and willingly, when others need our attention. It might mean we take time to listen. It could mean we share our food with others who are in need—or that we welcome others into our home when they need a place of comfort and safety. When we do all these things, God promises to bless us.

It's easy to focus on what you don't have. Your worries about finances or time can make you reluctant to share either with others. You may tell yourself that it's only right that you take care of yourself and your own family first. But God promises that if you take the risk of being generous, He will take care of your needs. He will bless you abundantly, in ways you may not expect.

Give me a generous heart, Lord. Make me more like You.

WHEN YOU LACK STRENGTH

They that wait upon the Lord shall renew their strength; they shall mount up with wings as eagles; they shall run, and not be weary; and they shall walk, and not faint.

Isaiah 40:31 KJV

Do you ever feel as though you simply don't have the strength to keep going? Maybe sadness is weighing heavy on your heart—or it could be that worry over money or a loved one's health is sapping your strength. It might be that you're physically exhausted, with responsibilities that take long hours. Whatever it is, the Lord wants to help. Not only can He give you the strength you need to keep going, putting one foot in front of the other, but He will give you the energy you need to *run*. He will even make you fly!

Oh Lord, You know that my strength has limits. Thank You that Your power is infinite. Please help me cope with the demands of my life. Show me if I need to say no to some of the responsibilities that weigh so heavily on me—and give me the strength I need to keep on serving You.

KEEP ON KEEPING ON

Blessed is the one who perseveres under trial because, having stood the test, that person will receive the crown of life that the Lord has promised to those who love him.

JAMES 1:12 NIV

Sometimes life is hard. There's just no way around it. And God never said anything different. Life will bring trials to all of us. It's inevitable.

But the Bible tells you that you're blessed if you don't give up. Keep moving. Put one foot in front of the other, and eventually you will come out the other side. Not only will God give you the strength you need to keep going, but He will also enrich your life. The Greek word translated "crown" means "that which surrounds." In other words, God will recognize your hard work and endurance by surrounding you with life, a life that's full, abundant, and joyful. And He always keeps His promises.

Give me the strength I need, Lord,
to keep going even when times are hard.

OBEDIENCE

If you listen obediently to the Voice of God, your God, and heartily obey all his commandments that I command you today, God, your God, will place you on high, high above all the nations of the world. All these blessings will come down on you and spread out beyond you because you have responded to the Voice of God, your God.

Deuteronomy 28:1–2 MSG

The Bible speaks of all manner of blessings. It would be hard to find a page in scripture that doesn't mention some way that God plans to bless His people. His love for us simply spills over into blessing!

But we can choose to put ourselves where God's blessings can no longer reach us. We can turn away from His path and choose our own way instead. At first, this may seem like a better way to get the things we want—but ultimately, it always leads to heartache, disappointment, and frustration.

God wants to lift you up high. He longs to fill your life with so many blessings that they spill over and spread out into the lives of everyone around you.

God, teach me to hear Your voice—
and give me the strength to obey.

LIKE A BIRD

"That is why I tell you not to worry about everyday life. . . . Look at the birds. They don't plant or harvest or store food in barns, for your heavenly Father feeds them. And aren't you far more valuable to him than they are? Can all your worries add a single moment to your life?"

MATTHEW 6:25–27 NLT

Even if you live in a city, you probably see at least one bird every day. Each time you see one of our feathered friends, let it serve as a reminder that just as God provides food for this small creature, He will also provide you with what you need to thrive.

Worrying is such an easy pit to fall into. We seem to think that by worrying we can somehow help shape the future. But as these verses remind us, worrying accomplishes exactly nothing. It's a useless spinning of our mental wheels—and it robs us of the peace and joy God wants us to experience.

Father, I give You all the details of my everyday life: food, clothing, money, bills, time—all of it! Teach me to be more like a bird, trusting You to supply all that I need.

SHARING

Now He who supplies seed to the sower and bread for food will supply and multiply your seed for sowing and increase the harvest of your righteousness; you will be enriched in everything for all liberality, which through us is producing thanksgiving to God. For the ministry of this service is not only fully supplying the needs of the saints, but is also overflowing through many thanksgivings to God.

2 CORINTHIANS 9:10–12 NASB

God asks us to reach out to others. He expects us to be His hands on earth, sharing generously with others. We have so many resources—money, skills, time, understanding, to name just a few—and God asks that we not hoard any of it. Our resources were given to us so that we could give them away. But He also promises that if you share what you have, you will have enough for yourself too. In fact, the Bible overflows with promises of God's care. Give whatever you can—and God will give back to you, richly, generously, bountifully.

Show me opportunities, Lord, to share my resources with others. Help me trust You to provide for me.

DO WHAT IS RIGHT

For the LORD God is our sun and our shield. He gives us grace and glory. The LORD will withhold no good thing from those who do what is right.

PSALM 84:11 NLT

You may have read about the law of attraction; a similar idea is referred to as the power of positive thinking. The basic premise of both is that if you focus your thoughts on something you want, the universe will give it to you. The Bible, however, says something different. It says to first do what is right. Surrender all your demands to God. Put Him first in your life, then love your neighbor as yourself (Mark 12:30–31). Let go of all your ideas about what you need to be happy. And then, when you do that, He will pour more blessings into your life than you can grasp. He won't hold back!

Thank You, Lord, for being my light and my protection. Thank You for giving me so much. Teach me to follow You. Give me a grateful heart.

THE FUTURE

"For I know the plans I have for you," declares the Lord, "plans to prosper you and not to harm you, plans to give you hope and a future."

Jeremiah 29:11 NIV

Does the future ever scare you? After all, you don't know what's coming. You can't predict what sorrows and losses lie ahead. On the other hand, you *do* know that the future will hold the inevitable losses of aging. People you love will die. As depressing as it sounds, it's simply the way things are.

But you don't need to live in fear. Through *everything* that comes, even the hard and painful things, God will be there right beside you. He has plans for your future—and you can trust Him when He says He wants you to be filled with hope. He will not let life destroy you. Instead, He will make certain that you prosper, through everything that happens.

Lord, when the future fills me with anxiety, bring to my mind the words of this verse. May I read it over and over, even commit it to memory, so that I always remember that You have my future in Your hands.

TRUSTING GOD

"Blessed is the man who trusts in the LORD, and whose hope is the LORD. For he shall be like a tree planted by the waters, which spreads out its roots by the river, and will not fear when heat comes; but its leaf will be green, and will not be anxious in the year of drought, nor will cease from yielding fruit."

JEREMIAH 17:7–8 NKJV

Trusting God blesses you. It frees you from anxiety and stress. It brings refreshment even during the most challenging of days. Even when you go through long stretches of hardship and trouble, you will continue to grow. Your life will still be productive, producing "fruit" that gives nourishment to everyone you encounter. God has blessed you with life that never ends!

Teach me, Lord, to trust You more and more. Thank You that my roots are sunk deep in Your life-giving river— and that my branches are heavy with the fruit of Your Spirit.

PRAYER

"Your Father knows exactly what you need even before you ask him!"

MATTHEW 6:8 NLT

The Bible tells us to "pray without ceasing" (1 Thessalonians 5:17 KJV). But if God already knows what we need, why do we need to pray?

You don't pray because God needs to be told what to do. You pray because you need to be in vital connection with God. You need to train your heart and mind to think in terms of the kingdom, rather than from the world's perspective—and prayer helps shape your thoughts so that they move in line with God's will for your life. You are blessed through prayer because God allows you to participate in His work.

Of course God already knows what you need, even better than you do yourself. You don't need to give Him directions as to how He should bless you! But He has given you the privilege of communicating with Him as often as you like. Why would you want to neglect such an amazing blessing?

I am glad, Father, that I can talk to You about my life and my concerns. Thank You that You are always listening.

ALL-INCLUSIVE

God's blessing inside the city, God's blessing in the country; God's blessing on your children, the crops of your land, the young of your livestock, the calves of your herds, the lambs of your flocks. God's blessing on your basket and bread bowl.

Deuteronomy 28:3–5 MSG

God's blessing on your life is all-inclusive. Everywhere you go, He is there with you. He blesses your children and the other people you love. He blesses your work and your possessions. He blesses you when you go to the grocery store and when you sit down to eat a meal. No aspect of your life is too small for Him to bless!

God, Your blessing on my life humbles me while also filling me with gratitude and joy. Teach me not to overlook one single blessing You have given me.

YOUR FATHER KNOWS YOU

"Your heavenly Father already knows all your needs. Seek the Kingdom of God above all else, and live righteously, and he will give you everything you need."

MATTHEW 6:32–33 NLT

Our needs can seem overwhelming. Often, we're far more aware of what we *don't* have, and we may overlook all that we do have. Whether it's money or time, physical abilities or social skills, artistic talent or external beauty, we often feel as though we just don't have *enough*. We feel lacking in so many ways.

But Jesus is saying in these verses that you are blessed because the Father knows your needs—and He will see that you have everything you need. Seek His kingdom first, and be confident that God has more than enough to give you. Trust Him to take care of you. Your heavenly Father understands you; He knows your life; and He will not forget to meet your needs.

Father, thank You for taking care of me.
Help me to always put Your kingdom first in my life.

RICH!

The blessing of the Lord makes a person rich.

Proverbs 10:22 NLT

The Hebrew word that is translated "makes rich" means "creates abundance." When we talk about the Lord's blessing, that's what we really mean: the abundant riches, thriving health, and overflowing bounty that God pours into our lives in countless shapes and forms, in myriad varieties, starting now and reaching into eternity.

This richness of life is what God's blessings create in your life. You may not ever become a millionaire, but you are truly rich because of the Lord's blessing.

Teach me, loving Lord, to be more aware of all the ways You enrich my life with Your blessings. May I not overlook a single one of the riches that You have poured into my life.

ENDURANCE

Let us run with endurance the race that is set before us, looking unto Jesus, the author and finisher of our faith.

HEBREWS 12:1–2 NKJV

Do you ever get tired of life's challenges? Do you ever long for a more carefree life, a life free from trials and trouble? Unfortunately, that isn't possible; each one of us will have to bear a certain amount of pain in this life.

But you can have a different perspective on the challenges that come your way. The Bible acknowledges that life can be hard, and it never promises that God's people won't have to learn to endure hardship and suffering. Through it all, though, God promises you His presence, love, and comfort. Jesus will walk beside you and give you strength to overcome whatever is in your path. You are blessed because Jesus will be with you—and one day, He will carry you across the finish line, into heaven's joys.

Give me strength to endure the challenges I face, Lord Jesus. Thank You that You not only are the source of my faith but will also complete my faith.

HOME AND CHILDREN

For he has strengthened the bars of your gates and blessed your children within your walls.

PSALM 147:13 NLT

God's blessing is not limited to you alone. It also reaches out into the world around you. And it includes the people you love, especially the children in your life.

In this verse, the psalmist's words assure us that God wants us to have secure homes—safe places for children to grow and be loved. God surrounds children with His love, doing whatever He can to help them grow strong. His love for these small people is even greater than ours is.

Lord, thank You for my home. May it be a place of blessing, a place where everyone who enters feels comfortable and safe. And I pray especially for the children in my life. May they feel Your presence with them and know that they are loved. Use me, I pray, to bless their lives—and continue to bless them when I am no longer around to show them my love.

BUTTERFLY

This means that anyone who belongs to Christ has become a new person. The old life is gone; a new life has begun!

2 CORINTHIANS 5:17 NLT

The monarch butterfly begins life as a green-and-black-striped larva. When the time comes, it makes itself a chrysalis. Inside that emerald-green container, the caterpillar is completely destroyed. Nothing is left of what it once was. If you were to cut open the chrysalis prematurely, you'd find nothing inside but a soupy liquid. And yet if you wait and leave the chrysalis alone, eventually an orange-and-black-winged butterfly will emerge.

You too have the potential to be transformed into a beautiful new creature. The process of spiritual metamorphosis is not always pleasant—but one day you will be blessed with wings to fly. You'll be what God intended you to be. Trust Him to see you through the transformation.

God, help me be patient with myself while You turn me into a new creature.

PRACTICAL BLESSINGS

God will order a blessing on your barns and workplaces; he'll bless you in the land that God, your God, is giving you.

DEUTERONOMY 28:8 MSG

Sometimes we think of blessings as things that exist only in the spiritual world—and it's true that God blesses us with spiritual gifts. He helps us love selflessly and gives us hope; He touches our emotions and calms our fears. But the Bible also speaks of physical blessings, practical gifts from God in the world we see and touch. This verse uses the word *barns*; in modern-day terminology, we might say our *bank accounts*.

As you give God more and more room in your life, He will bless your finances, your job, your home and possessions—your entire life. There is no aspect of your life that He will forget to bless!

God of blessing, thank You for all the ways You touch my life. I give You my bank account, my workplace, my home, and all my possessions. I trust You to bless me as You see fit.

THE POOR

Blessed are those who help the poor.

PROVERBS 14:21 NLT

"We think sometimes that poverty is only being hungry, naked and homeless," said Mother Teresa. "The poverty of being unwanted, unloved and uncared for is the greatest poverty." As you go through life, you will encounter all kinds of poverty—and God promises to bless you if you reach out to those in need. Whether people are hungry or hurting, the Bible says to give out of the overflow of love you have received from God. He will work through you as you serve food to those who are hungry, give clothing to those who need covering, offer hope to those who feel hopeless, and lend a listening ear to those who are lonely. And helping the poor will bless you as much or more than it does those you seek to help.

Show me opportunities to give to those in need, Lord. May I do so humbly, knowing that I am merely a vehicle for Your love. Help me to never be blind to the need of those around me.

WISDOM

If you need wisdom, ask our generous God, and he will give it to you. He will not rebuke you for asking.

JAMES 1:5 NLT

God has given us many sources of wisdom. We live in an age when information of all sorts is readily available to us online. We can read books and ask others for advice. We can listen to our own common sense. God can use all these things to guide us and inform us. But sometimes, none of these things are enough. No matter how many books and articles we read or how many people's advice we seek, we still feel bewildered and confused.

When that happens, take your questions to God. Don't be afraid to ask for His help. No question is too small or too big. He may direct you to a source of information you had overlooked. He might bring someone new into your life who has the wisdom you need. Or He could speak directly to your heart. However God chooses to communicate with you, He is the best resource you can find.

Generous God, give me the wisdom I need to live my life in a way that pleases You.

YOU CAN'T IMAGINE!

"No eye has seen, no ear has heard, and no mind has imagined what God has prepared for those who love him."

1 CORINTHIANS 2:9 NLT

Somewhere along the way, quite a few of us got the idea that anything we enjoy is a temptation to sin. It's true that anything we put ahead of God can become an idol, something we "worship" more than we do our Lord. But that doesn't mean the things we like most are sins in and of themselves.

All the good things in your life come directly from God. They are part of His plan for your life. He wants you to have a healthy relationship with these things. He wants you to enjoy His many blessings. In fact, He plans to bless you for all eternity. You can't even imagine all that He has in store for you.

God, I want You to be the Lord of my life. I give You all my joys and pleasures, knowing that You give them back for me to enjoy with Your blessing. Thank You for all that You have given me.

OPEN YOUR MOUTH

"I, the Lord, am your God, who brought you up from the land of Egypt; open your mouth wide and I will fill it."

Psalm 81:10 NASB

God is not tightfisted! He doesn't like to see you suffer, and He never holds back from blessing you. It makes Him happy to bless you in as many ways as you can imagine.

When you start to trust that God truly loves you that much, you can stop worrying so much. You don't have to lie awake worrying about bills; you can stop fretting over your family's health. Instead of stressing out every time you face a new challenge, you can praise God in each circumstance, knowing that it gives Him pleasure to bless you. Like a baby bird that has absolute trust in its mother, open your mouth wide—and God will fill it.

When I worry over my finances, Lord, remind me that You will care for me. When I fret over what will happen tomorrow, teach me that You hold tomorrow in Your hands.

YOU'RE STILL GROWING

I am certain that God, who began the good work within you, will continue his work until it is finally finished on the day when Christ Jesus returns.

PHILIPPIANS 1:6 NLT

Do you ever begin a project, fully intending to finish it, only to set it aside and leave it undone for. . .well, sometimes forever? We've all done that—but God does not. When He begins something, He finishes it.

God has been working within you ever since you were born. When you look back, you can probably see that He brought people into your life and shaped circumstances in ways that have helped you grow. So if you look at yourself and still see plenty of flaws and faults, don't feel discouraged. You are blessed because God is still working on you! And He won't stop until you are fully complete.

God, You know all my imperfections, even better than I know them myself. Thank You that You are patient with me. Thank You that You continue to help me grow.

COMING IN AND GOING OUT

God's blessing in your coming in, God's blessing in your going out.

Deuteronomy 28:6 MSG

Here is a blessing you can claim for yourself and your family every single day. As you leave the house for work or school, God will bless you. He will go with you and each member of your family as you go through the day; and then as you come home at the end of the day, He will still be with you. He will bless your family's coming back together. Going out and coming home, God will be with you. You are blessed through each moment of the day.

Thank You, God, for being with me each morning. Bless my family and me as we get ready for the day ahead. Go with us as we go our separate ways, and keep us safe. May we sense Your presence with us throughout the day. Thank You that You will be there when we come home, blessing our time together. Thank You that You are always with us.

GOD'S LOVE

Oh yes, people of Zion, citizens of Jerusalem, your time of tears is over. Cry for help and you'll find it's grace and more grace. The moment he hears, he'll answer. Just as the Master kept you alive during the hard times, he'll keep your teacher alive and present among you. Your teacher will be right there, local and on the job, urging you on whenever you wander left or right: "This is the right road. Walk down this road." You'll scrap your expensive and fashionable god-images. You'll throw them in the trash as so much garbage, saying, "Good riddance!"

ISAIAH 30:19–22 MSG

Our world is full of false ideas about who and what God is. The Bible says that God is love (1 John 4:8), and in these verses from Isaiah, we see God's love at work. When you cry, God will be there to comfort you. When you are overwhelmed and confused, He will teach you what you need to know, guiding you along paths that lead to life. You are so blessed to have this relationship with the one who created the world! He is not a faraway God who looks down on you with judgment and disdain; no, the Creator is a God of love.

God, I'm so glad You love me!

THE GOOD SHEPHERD

The LORD is my shepherd, I lack nothing. He makes me lie down in green pastures, he leads me beside quiet waters, he refreshes my soul.

PSALM 23:1–3 NIV

A shepherd has one job: to take care of his sheep. He makes sure they have enough to eat. He watches over their health and tends to their wounds and illnesses. He leads them to pastures where they can be nourished, and he brings them to rivers where they can drink and be cooled in the water.

Jesus spoke of Himself as the good shepherd, and He longs to do all these things for you. His entire focus is on you and your life, and He makes sure you have everything you truly need. Follow Him, and He will lead you to places of rest and refreshment. You are blessed because He cares for you so tenderly.

Jesus, thank You for being the shepherd of my life. I want to follow You wherever You lead. I trust You to care for me.

MERCY AND COMPASSION

Not returning evil for evil or reviling for reviling, but on the contrary blessing, knowing that you were called to this, that you may inherit a blessing.

1 PETER 3:9 NKJV

The Bible makes it clear that God cares how we treat others. He calls us to relationships that are based on love and compassion. As human beings, though, we often think that if someone is mean to us, we're justified in being mean in return. If someone talks about us behind our backs, we feel free to do the same. After all, it's only fair. God doesn't expect us to be doormats, does He?

No, He doesn't. But setting healthy boundaries is not the same as returning evil for evil. God calls you to interact with others in a radically different way than the world. No matter how you are treated, respond with mercy. Don't talk about others behind their backs. Be sure that all the words you speak are kind and uplifting.

And when you do these things, you will bless others—and you too will be blessed.

If I am tempted to retaliate when someone does or says something that hurts me, remind me, Lord, that You want me to reflect Your love.

NOURISHMENT

"You will have plenty to eat and be satisfied, and you will praise the name of the LORD your God, who has dealt wondrously with you."

JOEL 2:26 NASB

God wants you to be well nourished, both physically and spiritually. He doesn't want you to go hungry. So when you find yourself yearning for something more, take that feeling to the Lord. Ask Him to satisfy your longings as only He can.

When He does, don't forget to praise Him. Thank Him. Tell others what God has done for you. As you do so, you will make even more room in your heart for God's blessings and grace.

God is an amazing God—generous, loving, and kind. You can trust Him to bless you with the nourishment you need to thrive and be strong.

I praise Your name, God, for You have done so much for me. You see to it that I have everything I need. Thanks to You, I will never go hungry.

PARTICIPATING IN GOD

His divine power has given us everything we need for a godly life through our knowledge of him who called us by his own glory and goodness. Through these he has given us his very great and precious promises, so that through them you may participate in the divine nature.

2 PETER 1:3–4 NIV

God wants you to participate in His nature; He wants you to be part of His divine life. That may seem like an impossibility, and it would be from a human perspective. But God makes it possible through the blessings He has given you. In fact, He's giving you everything you need to live in line with His life. The more you get to know Him, the closer to Him you will grow, until your life merges with His.

Bring me closer to You, God. I want my life to flow into Yours.

SCRIPTURE

Whatsoever things were written aforetime were written for our learning, that we through patience and comfort of the scriptures might have hope.

Romans 15:4 KJV

When the apostle Paul wrote his letter to the Romans, the New Testament did not yet exist, so the scriptures he was referring to here are what we Christians now call the Old Testament. As you read the stories of Noah, Abraham, Sarah, Jacob, Joseph, Moses, Esther, Ruth, Job, David, Elijah, and many others, you will see that they were ordinary human beings. They made mistakes, and yet God comforted them in their darkest hours.

As you read these stories, take hope and comfort. God will help and guide you as He did these long-ago heroes of the faith. Their lives, with their examples of patience and courage, will comfort, teach, and encourage you. You will be blessed by scripture.

Thank You, Lord, for those who went before me, these men and women who loved and followed You. May I learn from their lives.

EXPANDED

The Lord shall increase you more and more, you and your children.

Psalm 115:14 KJV

God will bless you for eternity—but you don't have to wait to pass through death's door to experience His many blessings. He will expand your life right now, making it fuller, deeper, wider. In fact, He will give you a richer and more satisfying life than you ever thought was possible.

And this promise of abundant blessing isn't for you alone. The Lord's blessings are so great that they will spread out from you. They'll touch the lives of the children you love. God will expand their lives too, freeing them from the limits that sin and sadness would seek to impose.

The Lord's blessing has no limits.

Increase my life, Lord, so that it is big enough to contain all the blessings You want to give me. Expand my heart so that Your Spirit has room to dwell there.

THE SHADOW OF DEATH

Though I walk through the valley of the shadow of death, I will fear no evil; for You are with me; Your rod and Your staff, they comfort me.

PSALM 23:4 NKJV

Most of us are afraid of death. It's the great unknown. It's also the thing that separates us, sooner or later, from the people we love. Yet the Bible tells us that even here, God is with us. Each time death forces us to say goodbye, God will be close beside us, sorrowing with us and comforting our hearts. And whatever the end of our lives may hold, God will walk with us all the way through it—and out on the other side, into heaven's light.

You are blessed because you will never face death alone. The good shepherd will always be with you. His rod and staff will protect you, even in this darkest of all valleys.

Thank You, good shepherd, that I need never face death alone. Thank You that You are always with me, even in the shadows.

COMMITMENTS

Commit everything you do to the Lord.

Psalm 37:5 NLT

Whether it's a relationship or a volunteer effort, some of us find it hard to commit. Others overcommit, juggling too many things—family, friends, social events, work, church and community work, and spiritual time. Either way, God wants to help us, and as we give everything we do to God, He will be able to help us see where our commitments should be.

Ask God to help you balance your commitments in a way that is healthy for you. As you allow Him to be your guide, He will help you see when and where you should commit your time—and when and where you should say no. You will be blessed with a new freedom from stress, a peaceful sense that you are serving God by caring for both others and yourself.

I give my life to You, Lord—my work, my family time, my alone time. Teach me to commit wisely. Give me wisdom to see where I should give my time and energy.

GOD'S HANDS AND FEET

Never walk away from someone who deserves help;
your hand is God's hand for that person.

PROVERBS 3:27 MSG

The Bible reminds us that we are God's hands and feet. We carry His compassion to the world around us in practical ways. What a wonderful privilege and responsibility!

Ask God to open your eyes to the people around you who need His loving touch, His gentle encouragement, His compassionate intervention. You won't be able to meet all the needs you see, but if you ask Him, God will show you where you can make a difference.

And when you raise another's head, you raise your own as well. You will be blessed.

Loving God, I want to be Your representative on earth. Show me opportunities to reach out to others. May I be sensitive to others' needs.

CONFIDENCE

In quietness and in confidence shall be your strength.

ISAIAH 30:15 KJV

Confidence is really just the quiet assurance that you are enough—enough to get your work done, enough to be a good friend and family member, and enough to accomplish what God has called you to do.

For some of us, confidence comes easily, but for others, not so much. Sometimes we're self-confident in some situations but not in others. Lack of confidence can hold us back. It can keep us from doing the work to which God calls us.

If your confidence is lagging, reach out to God for help. He will help you unveil the real you—the confident and assured you, the you who is enough. He wants to bless you with confidence and strength!

Lord, increase my confidence, I pray. I don't want to let shyness or embarrassment hold me back from serving You.

INFINITELY STRONGER

You prepare a table before me in the presence of my enemies.

PSALM 23:5 NIV

We don't usually think of blessings being given to us when we're in the presence of our enemies—but that's what this verse promises.

Who is your enemy? Maybe it's a situation that is hard for you to handle. Your enemy could be a person, someone who seems to wish you harm, whether physical or emotional. Even your own emotions can be enemies, robbing you of the peace and joy God longs for you to have. Whoever and whatever are the enemies of your well-being and peace of mind, God is infinitely stronger than they are. He will give you the strength you need to overcome everything that fights against His will for your life. And in the meantime, even while those enemies seem to be unbeatable, He promises to bless you and feed you richly, in their very presence.

God, You know the enemies of my soul, the people, circumstances, and inner dilemmas I must face every day. Give me strength to meet these challenges—and thank You for blessing me even in the midst of them.

GRASPING FOR THE WIND

Better a handful with quietness than both hands full,
together with toil and grasping for the wind.
ECCLESIASTES 4:6 NKJV

This verse is talking about the sort of person who never has enough, who is always working harder and harder to get more. Maybe that person *will* end up with more, but is it worth all the stress? Wouldn't it be better to have less—and have time to enjoy your life?

Healthy ambition is fine, but when it comes to evaluating your life, God's scales weigh differently than yours do. Seen through His eyes, the smallest things can bring you the deepest joy. When you embrace your life just as it is, you can lay down the struggle to always get more and more. You can be blessed with contentment, knowing that this moment, just as it is, is complete.

When I stress over all the things I wish I had, remind me, Lord, that I have You—and You will take care of all my needs. I can rest in You. I don't want to spend my life trying to grab the wind!

HIGHWAYS TO ZION

Blessed is the person whose strength is in You,
in whose heart are the roads to Zion!

PSALM 84:5 NASB

Zion is God's special place, the city where His presence is real and living. So how wonderful it is to have roads within your heart that lead there!

This world tells you to be strong in yourself—but God says, "Be strong in Me. Don't try to do it by yourself. Let Me be your strength." When you have this kind of relationship with the Creator, you will be blessed, and you will have highways to Zion running through your heart. You can retreat into your own heart and find paths that lead you to the presence of the Lord. What's more, others who know you will also benefit from these highways. They'll learn from your spirit, finding their own heart ways to God.

Lord, be my strength. Teach me to depend more and more on You. Build Your roads in my heart, highways that will take me straight to You.

FROLICKING

"For you who revere my name, the sun of righteousness will rise with healing in its rays. And you will go out and frolic like well-fed calves."

MALACHI 4:2 NIV

This verse gives you a good picture of what it means to live in relationship with God. Revere God's name—in other words, value His identity more than all else—and light will shine on your life. That light will not only illumine your path; it will also heal all the old wounds you carry within your heart. You will be restored to health, spiritually and emotionally nourished, so much so that you will feel like playing again, the way you did when you were a child.

If you think the life of faith is the sort of life where you laugh seldom, think again. God wants you to frolic! He wants to bless you with light, health, nourishment, and a playful spirit.

I revere Your name, Lord. Shine Your light on me.
Heal me. Nourish me. Give me a child's heart.

VICTORY

[Jesus said,] "In the world you have tribulation, but take courage; I have overcome the world."

JOHN 16:33 NASB

We live in the physical world, the realm of reality that we can see and touch. At the same time, we are part of a larger realm, one that we can know only by faith while we are in this earthly life.

In the physical world, you, like everyone else, will face disappointments and struggles. But Jesus is asking you to trust Him and take courage from His words of promise. As a citizen of the kingdom of heaven, you are blessed with a greater power. You share in Jesus' victory over this world's death and disappointment. Jesus advocates for you in heaven. He walks beside you and cheers you on.

Jesus never claimed your life would be free from troubles—but He wants you to be assured that He has blessed you with eternal victory.

Jesus, thank You for overcoming the world on my behalf. May I take courage from Your presence with me.

OLD AGE

The righteous will flourish like a palm tree, they will grow like a cedar of Lebanon; planted in the house of the Lord, they will flourish in the courts of our God. They will still bear fruit in old age, they will stay fresh and green.

Psalm 92:12–14 NIV

Do you ever fear old age? We live in a society that is obsessed with youth, that acts as though each year we live past thirty is a mark of shame. Women are embarrassed to confess their age, and our elders are seldom honored and valued for their wisdom and experience.

But the Bible has a different perspective on aging. It promises you that you can flourish in old age. Although your body may lose abilities, your soul never has to stop growing. You will be blessed with a young heart that never grows old. Your life will continue to bear fruit; in other words, you will continue to be useful to the kingdom of heaven.

You don't have to fear old age!

When I get depressed by the passing years, Lord, remind me that You call me to an evergreen life, a life that remains rich and useful forever.

ROOTED

As you therefore have received Christ Jesus the Lord, so walk in Him, rooted and built up in Him and established in the faith, as you have been taught, abounding in it with thanksgiving.

COLOSSIANS 2:6–7 NKJV

Do you ever feel discouraged with your spiritual progress? It may seem as though you have to learn the very same lessons over and over—and you keep making the same mistakes again and again.

But you are blessed with roots that go down deep into Christ. No matter how things may look on the surface, beneath the soil, God tends your faith. The longer you follow Jesus, the deeper and stronger those roots will grow. God doesn't expect you to be perfect, and He doesn't care how many times He has to teach you the same lesson. He has infinite patience. Keep walking with Jesus, and trust that He's strengthening your roots beneath you.

I want to walk with You, Jesus. Build my faith in You. Give me deep roots. I am so thankful for our life together.

AT THE END OF YOUR ROPE

"You're blessed when you're at the end of your rope. With less of you there is more of God and his rule."

Matthew 5:3 msg

This verse seems counterintuitive. How can you be blessed when you're at the end of your rope? But that's what Jesus said. When you are stressed and overwhelmed, when you feel exhausted, when you don't think you can take another step—that's the very moment that God sends you a special blessing. You don't have to beat yourself up for not being stronger. God accepts you exactly as you are. Relax. Rest in Him.

So long as we think we have things covered, we may be shutting out God. But when we acknowledge that we can't handle our lives without help, that's the moment we give God freedom to act. We let go of our egocentric beliefs about ourselves, we release our tight grip on our lives—and we give God space to enter our lives.

"It's okay, beloved child," God says to you. "Let Me help you."

Thank You, Jesus, that when I am at the end of my rope, You are there, waiting to help.

LOVE AND LOSS

"You're blessed when you feel you've lost what is most dear to you. Only then can you be embraced by the One most dear to you."

MATTHEW 5:4 MSG

Jesus preached an entire sermon on blessings. (It's known as the Sermon on the Mount.) A lot of what He said must have been surprising to the people listening. He must have turned their ideas upside down. "How does that make sense?" they must have murmured to themselves when they heard Him say these sentences. "How can I be blessed if I've lost the thing I love the most?"

But so long as you depend on human beings for love and acceptance, you haven't begun to totally depend on God's love. Sooner or later, all humans will let you down, even if they don't mean to. When you're grieving, even death can seem like a betrayal.

That's the moment, though, that you can learn that God will never leave you, never fail you. His love is completely reliable, and He loves you more than any human ever could.

Thank You, Jesus, for Your unconditional love.

COMPLETE

"You're blessed when you're content with just who you are—no more, no less. That's the moment you find yourselves proud owners of everything that can't be bought."

MATTHEW 5:5 MSG

It's hard to be content with ourselves, especially when we receive a constant barrage of messages saying that we're not quite good enough. Advertisements and commercials are designed to convince us that we need *something* in order to be better (prettier, happier, cleaner, more popular). We look in the mirror, and so often our own reflections don't please us.

But Jesus says to you, "You are fine exactly the way you are. Be content with yourself—your body, your mind, your skills—because I love you exactly as you are. You don't have to try to be better. You don't have to look at others and wish you were more like them. Just be yourself, the person you were created to be."

Jesus, teach me to be content with who I am. Thank You that You have given me everything I need to be complete.

HUNGRY FOR GOD

"You're blessed when you've worked up a good appetite for God. He's food and drink in the best meal you'll ever eat."

MATTHEW 5:6 MSG

Way back in the fourth century, Augustine of Hippo wrote, "You have made us for Yourself, O Lord, and our hearts are restless until they rest in You." Augustine understood that there is a God-shaped hole within each of us. Without God, we can never be complete.

That sense of yearning emptiness can be uncomfortable. But in this verse Jesus said that the restless longing of our hearts is actually a blessing. Although we can never be completely satisfied in this life, the yearning for God will keep us ever growing, ever seeking to know Him better.

You are blessed when you are hungry for God!

Nourish me with Your Spirit, I pray, Lord. I long for You.

DON'T STOP CARING!

"You're blessed when you care. At the moment of being 'care-full,' you find yourselves cared for."
MATTHEW 5:7 MSG

It's hard sometimes to keep caring. Our hearts get tired. We want to shut down. We long to curl up in a little ball and hide from the world. Because caring hurts. Reading the news is painful, when there are so many stories about violence and hatred. It looks as though all our efforts are in vain. We're tempted to give up.

But God wants you to never quit caring. "Keep your heart soft," Jesus says to you in this verse. "Feel the world's pain and never stop trying to make a difference. And as you care for the world, I will care for your battered heart. Rely on Me."

Lord Jesus, give me the courage and strength I need to keep caring, even when the world around me seems so cruel and indifferent to the needs of others. Show me ways I can make even a tiny difference. Help me not to give up.

WITHIN AND WITHOUT

"You're blessed when you get your inside world—your mind and heart—put right. Then you can see God in the outside world."

MATTHEW 5:8 MSG

Sometimes we look around and it's hard to see the presence of God in the world. Instead, everywhere we turn we see polarization and discord; we hear voices arguing; we read cruel comments on social media. Peace seems far away from our world. How can God be present in such an atmosphere of hatred and distrust?

In this verse, Jesus says to you, "Worry about your inside world before you concentrate on the outside world. When your mind and heart are close to Me, you'll be able to see things differently. Dwell with Me in your heart—and you'll be blessed, because you'll be able to see Me more clearly in the outer world."

Show me, Jesus, anything in my heart that is not right with You. Clean out anything that stands between us. May I be sure that You are living within me—so that I can begin to see You more clearly in the world outside me.

PEACEMAKER

"You're blessed when you can show people how to cooperate instead of compete or fight. That's when you discover who you really are, and your place in God's family."

MATTHEW 5:9 MSG

We live in a deeply divided world. Each side sees reality in a totally different way from the other side. It's hard to even know how to communicate with each other. It can be tempting to just withdraw, to talk only to the people with whom we have things in common and to ignore everyone else. But the only way the deep divisions in our society can be healed is if we build bridges that reconnect us.

In this verse, Jesus calls you to be a peacemaker. "Help people get along," He says to you. "Demonstrate cooperation instead of competition. Let Me use you to heal your world. Don't be afraid to speak out in love—and I will bless you with a sense of security, the knowledge that you are doing My work."

Jesus, I pray that You would help me be a bridge builder and a peacemaker. It's hard to know where to begin—so please show me.

GOOD TROUBLE

"Count yourselves blessed every time people put you down or throw you out or speak lies about you to discredit me. What it means is that the truth is too close for comfort and they are uncomfortable. You can be glad when that happens—give a cheer, even!—for though they don't like it, I do! And all heaven applauds. And know that you are in good company. My prophets and witnesses have always gotten into this kind of trouble."

MATTHEW 5:11–12 MSG

The late Representative John Lewis once said, "Do not get lost in a sea of despair. Be hopeful, be optimistic. Our struggle is not the struggle of a day, a week, a month, or a year, it is the struggle of a lifetime. Never, ever be afraid to make some noise and get in good trouble, necessary trouble." Jesus' message in these verses is much the same. Don't be afraid to get in good trouble on behalf of the kingdom of heaven.

Lord, give me the courage I need to stand up for You and Your kingdom.

YOU'RE BEAUTIFUL

I will be like the dew to Israel; he will blossom like the lily, and he will take root like the cedars of Lebanon. His shoots will sprout, his majesty will be like the olive tree, and his fragrance like the cedars of Lebanon.

HOSEA 14:5–6 NASB

Look at all the ways God has promised to bless you! He will refresh you when your life feels dry; He will make your life burst into bloom. At the same time, you'll be sending down deep roots that will keep your life stable and steady. You will grow in new ways, no matter how old you are. You will be beautiful, inside and out. Your life will give off a sweet fragrance that others will breathe in. God loves you in so many ways!

Lord, I want to become the person You created me to be. Keep me always growing, deeper and taller, closer to You.

PLANS

We can make our plans, but the Lord determines our steps.

Proverbs 16:9 NLT

At first glance, this verse may seem a little discouraging. What's the point of making plans if God isn't going to cooperate with us?

But the author of this verse wasn't saying, "Don't make plans." Rather than drifting through life, it's always good to have a plan. Make your lists, set your priorities, write in your agendas, and work hard to accomplish your goals. But this verse reminds you to hold your plans lightly. Be willing to let them go if God guides you in another direction. Even the best plans may need to change—and sometimes what looks like a detour can actually lead you to a better way.

Surrender your plans to God. Ask for His help in filling out your agenda—and be flexible enough to change directions if He leads you down an alternate path.

I give all my plans to You, Lord. I want Your will for my life.
I know that You know what is best far better than I do.

SATISFACTION

The desires of the diligent are fully satisfied.

PROVERBS 13:4 NIV

We don't always get what we want in life. It's a hard lesson that every human has to learn. (That lesson is what makes the "twos" so "terrible.") Most of us no longer have a full-blown tantrum when things don't go our way, but it can still be hard to let go of something that we've set our hearts on.

The word translated as "desires" in this verse actually means "the substance or inner being of a person, the soul." This verse is promising that your deepest self, the inmost part of you, will be satisfied. You will be blessed with spiritual and physical nourishment. God promises. God knows better than you do what your soul truly needs!

Lord, help me trust You to meet my needs.
May I be diligent in seeking and following You.

BE STRONG!

"As for you, be strong and do not give up, for your work will be rewarded."

2 CHRONICLES 15:7 NIV

What is it that's threatening to make you lose your resolve and give up? Maybe it's exhaustion or discouragement. It might be niggling questions like, "Is this worth it? Is anyone going to notice?"

The Bible promises over and over again that your determination will be rewarded. God sees how hard you work, even if no one else does. He understands that you're tired sometimes; He knows you need some extra encouragement; and He says to you, "Be strong, beloved child. I'm on your side. Even if you can't always see the results of all your hard work, I see—and one day, when you cross into eternity, you'll be able to look back and see the fruit of all your labor. I am blessing all your efforts."

Give me strength, Lord God, to do the work You've called me to do. May I not depend so much on human approval or external results, but rather look to You for encouragement and approval.

FAITHFUL

Let us hold fast the confession of our hope without wavering, for He who promised is faithful.

HEBREWS 10:23 NKJV

People make promises, but they don't always keep them. Sometimes circumstances change, making it impossible for people to do what they intended. Other times, people simply change their minds. But God is faithful. The promises He's made He'll keep.

Sometimes life can mislead you into thinking your hope is lost. But if you can hold on, the shadows will eventually clear and you'll be able to see your path forward. You'll look back and see that God was always with you, working behind the scenes to make everything work out. You'll be blessed by the faithfulness of God, the one who will never let you down.

When my hopes seem to be dashed, give me the strength, Lord, to keep holding on to my faith in You. Thank You for all the promises in scripture. May I cling to them, knowing that You will be faithful to them all.

SEEKING THE LORD

Search for the Lord and for his strength; continually seek him.

Psalm 105:4 NLT

It's not always easy to see what God is doing in the world. We look around and see chaos. We ask ourselves why God allows so many disasters and so much destruction. At times, our spiritual lives can also seem empty and dry. God seems to be absent.

But this verse tells you that you'll be blessed simply by seeking God, even if you seem to be getting no answers. The medieval author Julian of Norwich wrote that the tension between seeking God and seeing Him is a normal aspect of the spiritual life. "It is God's will that we have three things in our seeking," she wrote. "The first is that we seek earnestly and diligently, without sloth, and, as it may be through His grace, without unreasonable heaviness and vain sorrow. The second is, that we abide Him steadfastly for His love, without murmuring and striving against Him. . . . The third is that we trust in Him mightily of full assured faith."

Lord, I seek Your presence, Your strength, Your love.
I pray that You will reveal Yourself to me.

A GOD WHO HEARS

You, Lord, hear the desire of the afflicted;
you encourage them, and you listen to their cry.

Psalm 10:17 NIV

Do you ever feel as though no one listens to you? Or if they do listen, they don't understand? It's easy to feel unheard in this life. Even those closest to you may sometimes fail to hear what you're trying to tell them. But God hears. He's never too tired, too busy, too distracted. You don't need an appointment. He's always listening, always encouraging.

So cry out to Him. Share everything with Him—those things that cause you pain, those things that bring you joy. Let Him in on your secrets and your hopes. You are blessed to have the Creator God as your best friend. He understands your desires, your hurts, and your joys, and He longs to encourage you.

Thank You, Lord, for being a friend who always understands. Teach me to rely on You and Your understanding so that I won't be as hurt if others don't hear the cries of my heart.

UNLIMITED POWER

"It is beyond my power to do this," Joseph replied. "But God can."

GENESIS 41:16 NLT

Human strength has limits. Emotionally, physically, and spiritually, there is only so far we can go before we run out of energy and resources.

But if you feel God leading in a particular direction, don't be too quick to say something is impossible! When you reach the end of your own strength, that's when God steps in. He can supply the resources, the skills, and the energy to accomplish amazing things. He has no limits!

God of power and might, thank You that I can call You my friend. I ask that You guide me to the projects and endeavors You want me to accomplish. Teach me to rely on Your strength rather than my own. May I never put limits on the work You want me to accomplish in Your name.

ETERNAL LIFE

"My sheep hear My voice, and I know them, and they follow Me. And I give them eternal life, and they shall never perish; neither shall anyone snatch them out of My hand."

JOHN 10:27–28 NKJV

A shepherd and his sheep live together so closely that they get to know each other well. The sheep can recognize the shepherd's voice, and the shepherd understands each of his sheep individually. They follow him because they know he will care for them and protect them.

Jesus wants to have a similar relationship with you. In eternity, you will have no need of protection, but here on earth, you inevitably face many hazards. Jesus, your good shepherd, is protecting you. He watches over you so that nothing and no one can keep you from reaching your destination—eternity. The life God has given you cannot be robbed from you. You have been blessed by His promise of eternal life.

Thank You, Jesus, for being the shepherd of my soul, for caring for me so tenderly. And thank You for the gift of eternal life.

FOOD FROM HEAVEN

He rained down manna upon them to eat,
and gave them food from heaven.

PSALM 78:24 NASB

The Israelites were going through a tough time. They had been wandering in the desert without a homeland, and now they lacked enough to eat. They began to grumble, and some of them wished they had never left Egypt, even though they had been slaves there. But God provided for His people. He sent them food from heaven to keep them from starving.

You may not encounter times of literal, physical starvation, but chances are good that at one time or another you'll experience spiritual or emotional hunger. You'll feel empty and yearning inside, lacking the nourishment you need to be happy and satisfied. When that happens, remember the Israelites' story—and expect to be blessed with "food from heaven."

Lord, remind me that You will always supply my needs. When I get impatient, teach me to trust You and wait for Your perfect timing.

GOD'S LOVE NEVER QUITS

God remembered us when we were down, his love never quits.
Rescued us from the trampling boot, his love never quits.
Takes care of everyone in time of need. His love never
quits. Thank God, who did it all! His love never quits!

PSALM 136:23–26 MSG

Do you ever feel as though life is trampling you under its heavy feet? No matter how hard you try, you just can't seem to get ahead—and every time you manage to get to your feet, something comes along to knock you down again.

In times like that, shout out God's name! Wait for Him to come to your rescue. He will not leave you helpless. You are blessed because God's love *never* quits.

Thank You, Lord of love, that You will never give up on me. Thank You that You hear me when I call. Thank You that Your love never quits.

RULED BY LOVE

For I command you today to love the Lord your God, to walk in obedience to him, and to keep his commands, decrees and laws; then you will live and increase, and the Lord your God will bless you in the land you are entering to possess.

Deuteronomy 30:16 NIV

God's blessings are many—but if you want to experience the full gamut of divine blessing, you'll need to be obedient to His commands. Jesus said that all the Bible's laws could be summed up by two commandments: to love God with all your heart, soul, mind, and strength; and to love your neighbor as yourself (Mark 12:30–31). That sounds simple, but what it really means is that God asks you to surrender your selfishness in order to serve Him and seek what's good for others. When you do those things, you will be blessed. You will grow into the person you were created to be, and you will enter into the life that God has planned for you.

Help me, Lord, to surrender more and more of my self-centered ego to You. I want my life to be ruled by love.

IN THE MORNING

In the morning, Lord, you hear my voice; in the morning I lay my requests before you and wait expectantly.

Psalm 5:3 NIV

When you make a habit of starting each day in prayer, you can face the day ahead in a state of expectation, excited to see what God will do for you today. It's not that you will always pray for a specific thing and get it, like placing an order online. But what you can expect, when you lay your concerns before God, is that He will hear you. He will be actively involved with your life. You can eagerly anticipate meeting Him throughout the day as you see His hand at work. So as you pray daily, you will be doubly blessed—both by your time of prayer and by the unfolding of events as God acts in your life.

I want to start each morning in Your presence, Lord—
and then I want to spend all the moments of the day walking
close to Your Spirit. I'm excited to see what You will do next.

FIRM IN THE FAITH

Be on your guard; stand firm in the faith;
be courageous; be strong. Do everything in love.

1 CORINTHIANS 16:13–14 NIV

Faith in Jesus is not something you commit to once and then don't think about again. It's a little like a marriage: A marriage may start with a wedding, but it takes a lifetime of daily dedication to make it work. Your relationship with God also needs attention and care, just as your human relationships do. You will need to guard your faith. You will need to be strong and courageous to keep going when times get rough. And you will need to learn to let go of your egocentric perspective and instead let love control your entire life.

Like all relationships, yours with God is a two-way street. As you learn to live in love, God's Spirit will alert you every day to possibilities and opportunities. Day by day you will see His faithfulness, and your faith will grow. Soon you will stop worrying about what is around the next corner. You'll know with certainty that your life is blessed because it belongs to God.

Jesus, I want to give my entire life to You. Show me if anything is coming between us. Point out any selfishness in my heart. Teach me to be more like You.

UNFAILING LOVE

Your unfailing love, O Lord, is as vast as the heavens;
your faithfulness reaches beyond the clouds.

PSALM 36:5 NLT

It's hard to imagine a love that never fails. As human beings, our love always has limits. But God's love is infinite, and His faithfulness is limitless. He won't abandon you. He won't walk away from you when you're in trouble. His faithfulness reaches farther than you can see or even imagine.

It's difficult to comprehend that kind of faithfulness when you live in a world full of disappointments. But you are blessed with God's never-changing presence and His steadfast commitment to you. His love is a reality you can depend on—and as a result, you can survive the disappointments of this life so much more bravely. God's faithfulness never fails!

I am so grateful, Lord, for Your unfailing love.

THE LAW OF THE LORD

Oh, the joys of those who do not follow the advice of the wicked, or stand around with sinners, or join in with mockers. But they delight in the law of the Lord, meditating on it day and night. They are like trees planted along the riverbank, bearing fruit each season. Their leaves never wither, and they prosper in all they do.

Psalm 1:1–3 NLT

Remember how Jesus summarized the "law of the Lord"? It's love—love for God and for others (Mark 12:30–31). This is what God asks you to ponder day and night, until love becomes the guiding force of your entire life. Separate yourself from this world's hatred and polarization. Don't let yourself get caught up in Facebook arguments; instead, focus on love in each post you make on social media.

And as you make love your polestar, the goal you aim toward in each thing you do, you will be blessed. Your soul will grow tall and strong, nourished by the Spirit, giving nourishment to all those around you.

Teach me, God of love, to always follow the example of Jesus. May I learn to love You more and more—and may I spread love to everyone I encounter.

MISTAKES

All glory to God, who is able to keep you from falling away and will bring you with great joy into his glorious presence without a single fault.

JUDE 24 NLT

All of us make mistakes. As human beings, we can't help but stumble and fall down, even when we're trying our hardest. Often, it's our own selfishness that trips us up. Sometimes, though, we have the best of intentions, and yet we still make mistakes.

But don't focus on your mistakes. As soon as you become aware that you've fallen short of God's plan for your life, give your failure to Him. His power will never be limited by any weakness of yours. He can bring good out of even your stumbles.

And in the end, when God welcomes you into eternity, He won't see a single fault in you. In His eyes, you'll be absolutely perfect.

Lord, You know how often I fail You. I give You my failures, asking that You work around them and through them. Help me do better in the future.

GOOD TIMES AND BAD

When times are good, be happy; but when times are bad, consider this: God has made the one as well as the other.

ECCLESIASTES 7:14 NIV

You may tend to think of God gratefully in the good times and ask for His help in the bad. But when you look around at your life and see pain and difficulty, that doesn't mean that God has lost control. He still has His hand on your life, He is still working, and He can bring good out of both good times and bad. Your feelings may tell you that everything is *awful*, but even as you struggle with your emotions, you can continue to trust God to work out His purpose in your life. He isn't bound by your feelings. He is bound by His commitment of love to you. And you are blessed because you need not be bound by your feelings either. Instead, you can rest on God's promises.

Help me, Lord, to learn to trust You even when times are hard, even when I struggle with my emotions. Give me confidence that You are always working in my life.

LIFE FOREVERMORE

The Lord bestows his blessing, even life forevermore.

Psalm 133:3 NIV

The Hebrew word that's translated as "life" in this verse is *chayah*, a word with a wide breadth of meaning that includes "to come to life in a new way; to be restored after being dead; to be healed; to be nourished; to recover from illness." Those are some pretty big blessings! And notice that the psalmist wrote in the present tense. He's talking about "life forevermore," but he's saying that God gives you that life now, in the present moment. You don't have to wait for eternal life because it starts right now. In this very moment, God is bringing you to life in new ways. He is restoring and healing the parts of you that have been broken, the parts that are ill and wounded, even the parts that seem dead. And He is nourishing you with His own being. You are blessed with life.

Living Lord, thank You for giving me life—right now and forever.

NO GREATER LOVE

"Greater love has no one than this, that a person will lay down his life for his friends."

JOHN 15:13 NASB

You may be lucky enough to have someone who loves you this much—enough to give his or her life on your behalf should there ever be a need for that. If so, you are blessed!

And you are also blessed because Jesus loves you this much. He gave away His whole self on your behalf. If there had been no other human being in the world besides you, Jesus still would have died on the cross, laying down His life so that you could be healed and whole. . .destroying death so that you could live forever with Him in eternity.

Jesus came to earth for *you* so that you could see and know how much God loves you.

Thank You, Jesus, for giving Your life for me. Thank You for loving me with all Your heart. Help me be the person You long for me to be.

THE PEACE OF JESUS

"Peace I leave you, My peace I give you; not as the world gives, do I give to you. Do not let your hearts be troubled, nor fearful."

JOHN 14:27 NASB

Jesus wants to share with you His own peace. That means you have access to the same peace of mind and heart He experienced during His life on earth. It's the legacy He left you, His going-away gift when He went back to His Father. You are blessed with peace.

When Jesus said, "Do not *let* your hearts be troubled," He was indicating that you have a choice in the matter. You can choose to dwell on fears and worries until they expand more and more inside your head. Or you can claim Jesus' gift of peace as your own. Today's psychologists agree—we can choose to shape our own thoughts. We don't have to let them run away with us. Each time a negative thought pops into your head, you can give it to Jesus, making room for His peace to fill your mind and soul.

Teach me, Jesus, to claim Your peace.
Thank You for sharing it with me.

LAVISH LOVE

See what great love the Father has lavished on us, that we should be called children of God! And that is what we are!

1 JOHN 3:1 NIV

God lavishes you with love because He Himself is rich with abundant love. In fact, the Bible tells us that God *is* love. Wherever love is present, so is God—and wherever God is, there is love.

Think about how delighted parents are to see their children opening presents on Christmas morning. That's how God feels about you. You are His child, and He longs to express His love to you in every way possible. Each of His blessings is a gift from Him, your heavenly Father, picked out just for you, because He loves you so much.

Thank You, Father, that I am Your child.
I appreciate the many gifts You have given to me.

INSEPARABLE

Who shall separate us from the love of Christ? Shall tribulation, or distress, or persecution, or famine, or nakedness, or peril, or sword? . . . Yet in all these things we are more than conquerors through Him who loved us. For I am persuaded that neither death nor life, nor angels nor principalities nor powers, nor things present nor things to come, nor height nor depth, nor any other created thing, shall be able to separate us from the love of God which is in Christ Jesus our Lord.

ROMANS 8:35, 37–39 NKJV

Nothing can separate you from Christ's love—not even you yourself. Oh, you can turn your eyes away from God. You can insist on ignoring Him; you can shut Him out of your life. But Christ's love never gives up. It leaks into the cracks of your heart. It waits patiently for you to turn around and notice it's there. It is always ready to bless you. If His love is stronger than death and life and all the powers of heaven, it's strong enough to overcome even you.

Lord Jesus, thank You that nothing can separate us from each other—not even my own shortcomings.

A THOUSAND GENERATIONS

Know therefore that the LORD your God is God; he is the faithful God, keeping his covenant of love to a thousand generations of those who love him and keep his commandments.

DEUTERONOMY 7:9 NIV

A thousand generations would be around thirty thousand years. Hundreds of thousands of people would be involved in those generations. Think of all the people in your family line going back through the centuries, individuals who suffered and rejoiced, toiled and sacrificed, lived and died. If just one of them had died without bearing children, you would not be here today. But God was with your ancestors, back through the countless generations. He was already blessing you thousands of years ago—and He will bless your descendants as well. He did not forsake your ancestors, and He will not forsake you or your children.

Thank You, Lord, for Your faithfulness that reaches across the years into the past and stretches into the future. Thank You that You were with my ancestors and that You will be with my descendants as well.

REPENTANCE

For the sorrow that is according to the will of God produces a repentance without regret, leading to salvation.

2 Corinthians 7:10 NASB

In the seventh century, John Climacus wrote, "To repent is not to look downwards at my own shortcomings, but upwards at God's love. It is not to look backwards with self-reproach but forward with trustfulness. It is to see not what I have failed to be, but what by the grace of Christ I might yet become."

Repentance doesn't need to be painful. You don't have to beat yourself up for mistakes you've made. Instead, repentance is a blessing—the birth of a new life. It leads to transformation and to salvation. The Greek word that is translated as "salvation" also means "well-being, safety, prosperity, deliverance from destruction." When you repent, you simply get back on track, back on God's path of blessing.

Show me, God, where I have gotten off track. Give me the courage to repent, so that I can be exactly who You want me to be.

SHARED LIFE

If we claim that we experience a shared life with him and continue to stumble around in the dark, we're obviously lying through our teeth—we're not living what we claim. But if we walk in the light, God himself being the light, we also experience a shared life with one another.

1 JOHN 1:6–7 MSG

People don't need to know much about the Bible or God to be able to tell if you're living a life of love, as Jesus told us to do. Living in close relationship with God spills over into your relationships with people. It empowers you to connect with people meaningfully. As you grow closer to God, you will find yourself growing in your relationships with others as well.

The apostle Paul wrote that in Jesus we are connected, the way the parts of a body are connected (1 Corinthians 12:27). Our lives are interdependent, united in Christ. At the deepest level, we share the same life.

So walk in the light—and you will be blessed by the life you share with others in Jesus.

Jesus, thank You that I am part of Your body.
May I contribute to the life of that body.

ANXIETY

Cast all your anxiety on him because he cares for you.

1 PETER 5:7 NIV

All of us have anxieties. They tend to circle endlessly through our heads, repeating their dreary little chorus of worry and fear. As author Jodi Picoult wrote, "Anxiety is like a rocking chair. It gives you something to do, but it doesn't get you very far." Indulging in worry is like running endlessly on a hamster wheel—we don't get anywhere, and in the process we rob ourselves of the peace and joy God wants us to experience.

But God understands, and He wants to help. "Give Me all your anxieties," He says to you. "You don't have to carry them anymore. I'll carry them for you. Let Me help. I love you. I want to bless you with peace of mind, freedom from anxiety."

Lord, when I let anxiety consume my mind,
remind me that You are ready and waiting to carry all my
worries. Thank You that You love me that much.

THE FATHER'S HAPPINESS

"It gives your Father great happiness to give you the Kingdom."

LUKE 12:32 NLT

When we pray to God, sometimes we sound as though we're talking to a tightfisted, not very nice authority figure. We plead with Him to give us the things we need. We beg Him to grant us our requests.

But you don't need to pray like that. You don't need to beg. You can pray with confidence, knowing that God is happy to bless you with all the riches of His kingdom. The kingdom of heaven is here and now, and it is wide and full, immense and beautiful beyond imagining—and God wants to give you the entire thing!

Father, thank You for being so generous with me. Help me trust You more and more to supply all my needs. Teach me to contribute in whatever way I can to Your kingdom here on earth.

UNIQUELY BLESSED

In his grace, God has given us different gifts
for doing certain things well.

ROMANS 12:6 NLT

God has blessed each of us with special talents and skills. That means that you too are blessed in this way!

Each of our gifts is necessary to God's kingdom. He blessed us with them for a purpose, so that we could use them to bless others. Sometimes we know our own gifts very well. Other times, we may need to ask a trusted friend or family member for help affirming what our gifts actually are. Some gifts may seem small—like the ability to be a good listener, having a loving nature, or being good at peacemaking—but these seemingly small gifts may actually be far more vital to the kingdom of God than more obvious gifts like being good at singing, artwork, or writing.

Lord, thank You for blessing me with special skills.
May I not be shy about using them to build Your kingdom.

LIMITLESS!

Be glad, people of Zion, rejoice in the L*ORD your God. . . . He sends you abundant showers.*

JOEL 2:23 NIV

God loves to give His blessings to us. As human beings, we may like to give gifts to those we love—but our ability to give has limits. Financially, emotionally, spiritually, we can only give so much, and then we run out of resources. God's bounty, however, has no such limits. He gives abundantly, moment by moment, day by day.

Learning to see God's blessings showered throughout your day can be like a game you play with Him. The more you look for them, the more you'll find, for our abundant God is limitless in His blessings. You are lavishly blessed!

Thank You, heavenly Father, for showering my life with blessings. Teach me to see Your generous hand at work in my life.

INNER GRACE AND PEACE

May God give you more and more grace and peace.

1 Peter 1:2 NLT

God's blessings are not only external. He also blesses our inner spirits. Of course, we all have emotional ups and downs. And according to Mental Health America, about one in every eight of us will experience a serious depression at some point in our lives. But even in the midst of emotionally dark days, we can still experience the grace and peace of God. Our emotions may go up and down—but God's blessing never does. His grace and peace are constants we can depend on, even in the midst of depression, anxiety, or heartache.

Lord, when my heart is heavy, remind me that You are still blessing me with Your grace and peace. Even if I can't feel them, I know they are there. Please heal my hurting heart.

BEFORE THE CREATION OF THE WORLD

How blessed is God! And what a blessing he is! He's the Father of our Master, Jesus Christ, and takes us to the high places of blessing in him. Long before he laid down earth's foundations, he had us in mind, had settled on us as the focus of his love, to be made whole and holy by his love. Long, long ago he decided to adopt us into his family through Jesus Christ. (What pleasure he took in planning this!) He wanted us to enter into the celebration of his lavish gift-giving by the hand of his beloved Son.

EPHESIANS 1:3–6 MSG

God loves to bless you. You are the focus of His love. Even before He created the world, He had you in mind, and He was already planning the ways He would bless you. Now, just as His Son is blessed, you are as well, for you too are a child of God. He longs to lift you up to the high mountains of blessing, the places where you'll be able to receive more and more of His generous love.

God, I can't comprehend how much You love me. A love that has existed for eternity—and is all mine!—is just too great to wrap my head around. So all I can say is thank You.

DELAYED HOPE

Delayed hope makes the heart sick, but fulfilled desire is a tree of life.

PROVERBS 13:12 HCSB

Many of the women who fought for women's rights never got to see the results of their lifelong work. The same is true for those who fought to end slavery. They must have felt discouraged at times; they must have been sick at heart. And yet they kept on working to bring about change, change that today we get to experience.

In our day, we too are called to work for justice. It can be easy to get discouraged, but we need to see things from God's perspective. In the light of eternity, all our hearts' desires are already met. We are fully blessed right now. And because we are, we can be strengthened to plant trees of life that those in the future will one day enjoy.

When all my hopes seem to come to nothing, Lord God, remind me that You are working for eternity. Help me see with Your eyes and trust that my hopes will be fulfilled in Your perfect timing.

WORKDAY BLESSINGS

Commit your works to the L*ORD*, *and your thoughts will be established.*

PROVERBS 16:3 NKJV

God has called you to do some work in this world. Whether it's the work you do at a job or the work you do caring for a household (or both), God longs to be a part of it. This is also an area of your life that He longs to bless. As you start your workdays by giving each aspect of your work to God, you make room for Him to come into your work and bless you and the world around you. All it takes is a few moments of mental prayer as you begin to work. If you make this a habit, you'll find that you can be more focused ("your thoughts will be established"). You may be surprised by all you can accomplish!

Thank You, Lord, for being interested in each aspect of my life. I want to make more room for You so that You can bless me more and more. Take my work life and make it Yours.

STAND YOUR GROUND

With all this going for us, my dear, dear friends, stand your ground. And don't hold back. Throw yourselves into the work of the Master, confident that nothing you do for him is a waste of time or effort.

1 CORINTHIANS 15:58 MSG

With so much turmoil in our world, it can seem nearly impossible to stand our ground. We feel pushed back and forth from all sides. It can seem as though the best thing to do is retreat, back into our shell, back into our own little world.

But God doesn't want you to retreat. He wants you to throw yourself out there, working for Him in whatever way He calls you. Even when it seems as though all your effort is going nowhere, you can still be confident, resting in the knowledge that He will take your efforts and bless them. Your work for God not only blesses others; it also blesses your own heart, mind, and body.

Lord, show me the work You want me to do—and then give me the confidence I need to give it my heart and soul.

INNER BEAUTY

What matters is not your outer appearance—the styling of your hair, the jewelry you wear, the cut of your clothes—but your inner disposition. Cultivate inner beauty, the gentle, gracious kind that God delights in. The holy women of old were beautiful before God that way.

1 PETER 3:3–5 MSG

Our world is full of messages about how we should look. Everywhere we turn, we're told we need to have a body that looks a certain way. In order to meet with the world's approval, we need to wear particular kinds of clothes and style our hair in specific ways. There's nothing wrong with taking care of our bodies or being fashionable—but this is not where we are to find our identity.

You are blessed, no matter what you look like. Your true beauty comes from the inside.

Gracious God, thank You that You love me just the way I am. May I be beautiful in Your sight.

YOUR ESSENCE

"The Lord does not look at the things people look at. People look at the outward appearance, but the Lord looks at the heart."

1 Samuel 16:7 niv

You are blessed because God sees who you truly are, the whole you. He doesn't judge you by any external quality you have or don't have. He doesn't care if you're outgoing or shy, if you're a good singer or can't carry a tune, if you were good in school or struggled to get good grades, if you're a rebel or a peace lover, if you make people laugh or struggle to even raise a smile, if you're fat or thin or somewhere in between, if you're up on the latest fashion or wear whatever old thing you find in your closet. None of that matters to God! He sees the "you" who is deep inside, the very essence of who you are—and He loves you.

Thank You, God, for Your unconditional love.

THE ARMOR OF GOD

Be strengthened by the Lord and by His vast strength. Put on the full armor of God so that you can stand against the tactics of the Devil. For our battle is not against flesh and blood, but against the rulers, against the authorities, against the world powers of this darkness, against the spiritual forces of evil in the heavens. This is why you must take up the full armor of God, so that you may be able to resist in the evil day, and having prepared everything, to take your stand.

EPHESIANS 6:10–13 HCSB

Our world is often a frightening place. But you don't have to face the world defenseless. You are blessed because God not only gives you access to His vast strength, but He also offers you His armor to wear. The real battle isn't against the external dangers of this world but rather against attitudes and emotions, against the darkness in the spiritual realm. With God's help, wearing His armor of love, peace, and hope, you'll be ready to stand up for God, no matter how scary the world may seem.

When the world scares me, Lord, remind me to put on Your armor. Thank You that You have promised to defend my heart.

AGING

When my skin sags and my bones get brittle,
God is rock-firm and faithful.
Psalm 73:26 msg

We care what we look like, and we dread getting old because our appearance will change. It's okay to take pleasure in our appearance, but our deepest identity does not rely on external qualities.

You are blessed because no matter how old you get, no matter how saggy your skin or gray your hair, God never changes. His faithfulness was with you when you were a baby, it has continued with you through all the changes the years have brought, and it will be with you as you age. When He looks at you, He sees a soul as bright and shiny and beautiful as the day you were born.

Lord, help me not to dread aging. Teach me that true beauty is mine no matter how old I get.

YES!

Whatever God has promised gets stamped with the Yes of Jesus. In him, this is what we preach and pray, the great Amen, God's Yes and our Yes together, gloriously evident. God affirms us, making us a sure thing in Christ, putting his Yes within us. By his Spirit he has stamped us with his eternal pledge—a sure beginning of what he is destined to complete.

2 Corinthians 1:20–22 MSG

Do you ever feel that following Jesus means saying no to a lot of things? The reality is that with every no comes a yes. Jesus is all about yes—and He says yes to you, to your very being. He created you to be a specific person, like no other, and again and again He affirms His creation. With every moment, He is helping you reach the fullness of your true identity. You are blessed because God affirms your very being!

Teach me, Jesus, to rely more on Your yes—and care less about what the world thinks. Give me confidence in Your love.

THE LIKENESS OF GOD

In reference to your former way of life, you are to rid yourselves of the old self, which is being corrupted in accordance with the lusts of deceit, and that you are to be renewed in the spirit of your minds, and to put on the new self, which in the likeness of God has been created in righteousness and holiness of the truth.

EPHESIANS 4:22–24 NASB

You are blessed because your real self is made in the likeness of God. Imagine that. You carry within you the image of God.

When we live without God, turning away from His love, we are being false to that true self, the God image we carry in our deepest souls. Old habits can die hard, and it may take some effort to live in a new way. That old false self may keep calling to us. But with God's help, we can be renewed daily into God's own image.

God, I want to look like You. I want to act like You. Put my old false self to death, and help me be the person You created me to be.

THIRSTY

"Anyone who is thirsty may come to me! Anyone who believes in me may come and drink! For the Scriptures declare, 'Rivers of living water will flow from his heart.'" (When he said "living water," he was speaking of the Spirit, who would be given to everyone believing in him.)

JOHN 7:37–39 NLT

Sometimes we feel dry and empty inside. We're thirsty for something we may not even be able to name. When you feel like that, Jesus wants to refresh you. He wants you to open your heart to His Spirit so that He can quench your thirst. His well of living water is bottomless; you can drink your fill, every day, because you can never exhaust its supply. He always has more to give.

You are blessed because you have the Spirit—living water—flowing into your heart from Jesus. Let it flow into you—and then out of you into the world around you.

Jesus, thank You for Your living water.
Remind me today to drink my fill from Your Spirit.

LIGHT

Your word is a lamp for my feet, a light on my path.

PSALM 119:105 NIV

Life can seem pretty dark. Not only is our world full of danger and discord, but we can also become confused by all the choices out there. Should we do this? Or should we do that? Some days, even the smallest choices can be overwhelming. We feel confused, bewildered. We long for clarity. We want to do the right thing—but it's hard to sort out what that is when so many conflicting messages bombard us.

But you are blessed because God shines His light on your path. His Word—the Bible and Jesus—are lights you can rely on, even in the most confusing level of darkness. Be patient. Don't take action until you see God's light shining. He will show you the way to go.

Lord of love, I feel so confused about life some days.
Teach me to rely less on others' opinions—and more on Your light.

FREELY AND LIGHTLY

"Are you tired? Worn out? Burned out on religion? Come to me. Get away with me and you'll recover your life. I'll show you how to take a real rest. Walk with me and work with me—watch how I do it. Learn the unforced rhythms of grace. I won't lay anything heavy or ill-fitting on you. Keep company with me and you'll learn to live freely and lightly."

MATTHEW 11:28–30 MSG

Do you ever feel as if somewhere along the way you misplaced your real life? In the midst of all the busyness and stress, you somehow lost touch with the goals and ideas that once shaped you. You'd love to find your way back—but you're so tired, so overwhelmed with responsibilities. Jesus understands. He says to you, "You're blessed because I love you—and I want to lift your heavy burdens off your shoulders."

Following Jesus does not mean taking on a new set of burdens. Instead, it means finding a way of life that is truly comfortable, that fits the shape of your soul. In Jesus, you can find rest for your soul.

Jesus, I want to keep company with You.
Teach me Your way of living—freely and lightly.

THE LAW OF CHRIST

Bear one another's burdens, and so fulfill the law of Christ.

GALATIANS 6:2 NKJV

What is the law of Christ? Jesus told us what it is in Mark 12:30–31: to love God with all our heart, soul, and mind, and to love others as ourselves. This law of love is at the center of everything Jesus taught. It sums up the Bible's message in a nutshell.

And you are blessed because Jesus calls you to participate in His kingdom of love. You can be a conduit of love. One way you can do this is by bearing others' burdens—taking time to listen, to pray, and to reach out a helping hand in any practical ways that come along. Carry in your heart those who are hurting—and so fulfill the law of Christ.

Jesus, teach me to see opportunities to share Your love.
Show me those who are carrying heavy burdens—
and help me do whatever I can to lift their load.

CHALLENGES

Because the Sovereign Lord helps me, I will not be disgraced. Therefore have I set my face like flint, and I know I will not be put to shame.

ISAIAH 50:7 NIV

Life is full of challenges. Each day seems to bring a new set. Some people have learned to head into challenges with their heads high, enjoying the thrill—while others would rather curl up in a ball and hide their heads. Most of us probably have days when we're up for a good challenge and days when we feel too tired and overwhelmed to face one more thing. Either way, God is with us.

You are blessed because the Sovereign Lord helps you with the challenges of your life. You don't have to worry about being embarrassed or falling flat on your face. Whether your efforts succeed or fail by the world's standards, from God's perspective you will never be put to shame. With His strength, you can face any challenge.

Sovereign Lord, give me the strength I need to face each challenge today. I know that with Your help, I will not be put to shame.

FRUITFUL

"I will bless him, and make him fruitful."

GENESIS 17:20 NASB

The Hebrew word in this verse that has been translated "bless" refers to making something bear fruit. You are blessed because God makes your life productive. You have the ability to create a home, to accomplish all different kinds of work, and to express yourself in sewing, writing, gardening, music, or some other art form. That's one kind of fruitfulness God has given you. He also makes your spirit bear a different kind of fruit, the fruit of the Spirit—joy, humility, peace, understanding, and most of all, love. Not only are you blessed, but the fruit of your blessedness will bless others too!

Lord, I want my life to bear fruit that pleases You.
May each thing I do be a blessing to others.

THE SPIRIT'S BLESSINGS

The Spirit is poured on us from on high, and the desert becomes a fertile field, and the fertile field seems like a forest. The L*ORD's justice will dwell in the desert, his righteousness live in the fertile field. The fruit of that righteousness will be peace; its effect will be quietness and confidence forever. My people will live in peaceful dwelling places, in secure homes, in undisturbed places of rest.*

ISAIAH 32:15–18 NIV

These verses have beautiful words of blessing to unpack. As the Spirit pours down on us, the dry places in our lives become fertile; they burst forth with life. God's justice is simply the way He does things: fairly. Without favoritism. Ordering all things according to His loving nature. Creating peace, quiet confidence, and a sense of security in our lives. The Hebrew word for peace—*shalom*—has a deeper meaning than our English word. It's more than freedom from conflict; it also means health and completion, well-being and safety.

You are blessed with all these things: fruitfulness, peace, well-being, health, confidence, safety, security, rest—and most of all, the Spirit.

Spirit, thank You for pouring Your blessings into my life.

GOD IS OUT IN FRONT

"Go in peace; your way in which you are going has the LORD's approval."

JUDGES 18:6 NASB

In this verse, "peace" means "freedom from fear." What a wonderful promise: You can proceed through your life without fear. Although most of us don't often fear for our physical lives, our world is full of other dangers. Oftentimes, as we think about our world, with all its illnesses, turmoil, and political strife, we allow our hearts to be overwhelmed with anxiety. We worry for ourselves and our loved ones. We fret over how things will turn out. But when this verse says that your way has the Lord's "approval," the literal meaning in the original language is "to go in front of."

In other words, God is preceding you. He holds the future in His hands. He knows how things turn out—and He doesn't want you to be afraid. You are blessed because you can live your life free from anxiety.

Comfort my heart, Lord, when my worries threaten to overcome me. Increase my trust in You.

BURSTING WITH LIFE

Shout for joy to the Lord, all the earth, burst into jubilant song.

Psalm 98:4 NIV

In this verse, the Hebrew word *patsach*, which has been translated as "joy," means "to make something burst open, to break forth into new life." Imagine a spring day, when green buds are opening on every twig, and every bird and frog and bug is singing at the top of its lungs. That's the sort of joy that God has blessed you with, the sort of joy that can't be contained. It will break open the hard areas of your heart, letting joy and life spill out of you into the world. It will burst through all the barriers that have been holding you back, everything that's been standing in your way and keeping you from being the person you were created to be. This is the sort of joy that will make you grow.

Lord, my soul shouts for joy to You.
Teach me to sing Your song of gladness and growth.

GOD AS YOUR TEACHER

I will instruct you and teach you in the way which you should go; I will advise you with My eye upon you.

PSALM 32:8 NASB

We don't often hear God speaking to us clearly and directly. He doesn't shout His directions into our ears (though we may wish He would). Instead, He uses circumstances to guide us. He may use other people in our lives to help us see which way is right for us. We may have an inner sense that God is leading in a specific direction.

This verse says that God promises to teach you. Teaching isn't a one-and-done sort of thing. It's generally a long, slow process. But God has promised to be both your teacher and your counselor. He is your guide on the path of life. You are so blessed!

Thank You, Lord God, for teaching me, counseling me, and guiding me. Make Your directions clear to me, I ask.

SPIRITUAL EARS

Whether you turn to the right or to the left, your ears will hear a voice behind you, saying, "This is the way; walk in it."

ISAIAH 30:21 NIV

Wouldn't it be nice if you could actually hear God's voice whispering in your ear which way He wanted you to go?

That's not the way God works, though, at least not for most of us. Instead, we need to practice sharpening our spiritual ears. The world is so full of noise, so full of messages coming at us from all directions, and all that noise can drown out the still, small voice of God (1 Kings 19:12). We may need to discipline ourselves to spend times in literal silence, including online silence, so that we have opportunities to learn to hear how God is leading us.

If you want to hear God's voice, you need to listen with the ears of your spirit. And then He will bless you with the guidance you need.

Thank You, Lord, that You have promised to guide me.
Give me times of silence so that I can learn to hear Your voice.

UNFAILING LOVE

I am like an olive tree, thriving in the house of God.
I will always trust in God's unfailing love.

PSALM 52:8 NLT

All children need love to thrive—and we older folks are no different. Without love, our hearts would be miserable and lonely. Our lives would be narrow and unfulfilling.

In fact, love is the most important of all the many blessings God gives to you. All His blessings, both the spiritual ones and the earthly ones, are expressions of His love. You are blessed because God loves you. And He will never stop blessing you, because His love never fails. You can trust Him!

God, I want to live in Your house forever. I know that it's the place where I'm the happiest, where I can grow and be strong. Thank You for loving me so much.

SHADOWS

"The people living in darkness have seen a great light; on those living in the land of the shadow of death a light has dawned."

MATTHEW 4:16 NIV

Do you ever feel as though you're stumbling around in the dark? You'd like to follow God, but stress, sadness, worries, and frustration overwhelm you. You're so confused that you don't know which way to turn.

People had these same feelings when Jesus was on the earth. And Jesus understood and wanted to help. In this verse, He promised that His light will dawn even in the darkest night. You are blessed because Christ's light will rise in your life—and when it does, all the shadows will disappear. Jesus said He'd do that for you!

Jesus, thank You that You can see through the shadows in my life. I'll keep following You through the darkness—until Your light drives the night away.

DEEP PEACE

And He said to her, "Daughter, your faith has made you well; go in peace and be cured."

MARK 5:34 NASB

In the New Testament, which was originally written in Greek, the word that's been translated as "peace" was *eiréné*. This is a beautiful word with a great depth of meaning. It is a type of peace that knits all the essential parts of our lives together, so that everything is in harmony. All the broken pieces of our hearts are healed. Everything is exactly as it should be, with all the beauty that God intended. That is what Jesus promised in this verse.

You can choose to turn away from God—but why would you want to? Your faith in God has the power to heal you. You will be blessed with a deep peace that reaches down to the very bottom of your being.

Jesus, thank You for the peace and healing You offer me. Increase my faith so that I can become exactly the person You intend me to be.

WHAT'S GOOD FOR YOU

This is what the Lord says—your Redeemer, the Holy One of Israel: "I am the Lord your God, who teaches you what is good for you and leads you along the paths you should follow."

Isaiah 48:17 NLT

Do you ever feel unwilling to ask the Lord for His guidance? Maybe you feel that He'll ask you to do something you don't want to do. You might think He'll say no to something you really want to do.

But that's not the way God works. He wants to say yes to you! He wants only what is good for you, all the things that will truly give you health, happiness, and wholeness. If He says no, it's because He knows that a particular path leads to something less than His perfect plan for your life. It may even lead to pain and heartache that He longs for you to avoid. God's guidance always is a yes to life, to joy, to love, to blessing. Trust Him!

Lord, teach me what is truly good for me.
Show me the paths that will lead me to You.

HOME

"Just as the Father has loved Me, I also have loved you; remain in My love."

JOHN 15:9 NASB

Imagine that! Jesus loves you just as much as His heavenly Father loves Him! Think about it. The Son of God, the Word that existed from before the beginning of the world, who was present when the world was created . . .that same Jesus loves you, infinitely, utterly, with all His heart. How blessed you are!

And when Jesus asks you to "remain" in His love, He's saying, "Make My love your heart's home. Be comfortable there. Live there. Come back there whenever you stray. Know that you are secure there." You are so blessed to have Jesus' love as the home where you can dwell forever.

Jesus, I can hardly believe that You love me so much. All I can say is thank You—thank You for loving me; thank You for giving me Your love, where my heart can be at home.

REFUGE

The Lord *also will be a refuge for the oppressed,*
a refuge in times of trouble.

Psalm 9:9 KJV

When the psalmist used the word *refuge*, he was talking about a stronghold on a high mountain, a castle or fort that was defended against enemies. This wasn't a fairy-tale castle, but a practical defensive site. From its high vantage point, guards could see far in the distance so that they'd know in advance if enemies were approaching.

That's the sort of refuge God offers you. When life is hard, when people don't understand you, when troubles come, you can run away to His stronghold. You are blessed because the Creator of the universe will protect you, even in the midst of danger.

Thank You, Lord, for being my refuge.
Remind me to flee to You whenever dangers approach.

ENEMIES

You prepare a feast for me in the presence of my enemies. . . . My cup overflows with blessings.

PSALM 23:5 NLT

This is another one of those Bible verses that doesn't make sense at first glance. We think of blessings as things we experience in happy times, when life seems good—not when we're surrounded by enemies. And yet the Bible promises that this is the very situation where God will lay out a feast for us to eat.

Your enemies may come in various shapes and forms. They could be your emotions that threaten to overcome you with depression, anxiety, or anger. They might be other people who give you a hard time, either at home, at work, or in your community. Your enemies could be spiritual forces, or they could be destructive forces in our society. The psalmist didn't specify what kind of enemy. But he did promise that God is blessing you even in the midst of troubles—so much so that your cup will overflow!

God, when I feel as though I'm surrounded by enemies, remind me that even then, You are blessing me.

JESUS

This is how God showed his love among us: He sent his one and only Son into the world that we might live through him.

1 John 4:9 NIV

Sometimes God's love can seem too intangible to touch. But that is why God sent His Son to live with us—so that we could see exactly what God's love looks like. When our hearts are sad, we don't have to try to grab hold of something that's too "spiritual" to understand. God sent His love to us in the physical body of Jesus. Jesus was the love of God walking on earth.

God blesses you in so many ways; He expresses His love through all the many, many good things in your life. But the ultimate expression of His love is Jesus. Because Jesus came to live in this world, you are blessed. You have a new life through Him.

Jesus, thank You for coming to earth to show us what the love of God looks like.

ENDURANCE, STRENGTH, AND CONFIDENCE

We can rejoice, too, when we run into problems and trials, for we know that they help us develop endurance. And endurance develops strength of character, and character strengthens our confident hope of salvation. And this hope will not lead to disappointment. For we know how dearly God loves us.

ROMANS 5:3–5 NLT

Athletes know that when they push their bodies, putting stress on them, their bodies' muscles grow stronger and their endurance increases. Athletes head into competition with confidence in their bodies' abilities because they know that their bodies are in peak condition, thanks to weeks and months of practice.

The Bible promises you so many good things—but it never says that troubles won't come your way. Instead, it says that you too, like an athlete, can build endurance, strength, and confidence as you live through problems and trials. Hard times won't destroy you. Instead, you will be blessed in ways you may never have expected.

Remind me, God, that even in the midst of hard times, Your love is with me, helping me grow strong.

GOD'S CREATURES

O L*ORD*, *what a variety of things you have made! In wisdom you have made them all. The earth is full of your creatures.*

PSALM 104:24 NLT

Sparrows and dogs, minnows and turkeys, elephants and chipmunks, frogs and giraffes, earthworms and whales—the earth is full of creatures that God has made in His wisdom. We live in a world rich with variety and beauty. As Robert Louis Stevenson said, "The world is so full of a number of things, I'm sure we should all be as happy as kings." The natural world reveals to us the Creator's hand. It feeds us, inspires us, entertains us, and comforts us.

You are blessed to live in a world that is so full of plants and animals, so overflowing with beauty and life.

Lord, thank You for Your creation. May I honor it and protect it.

GOD'S COVENANT

I give unto him my covenant of peace.

NUMBERS 25:12 KJV

When God talks about a covenant, He's referring to a binding promise that can never be broken. Human beings make promises—and even with the best of intentions, they often break those promises. But God's promises are not like that. When He says He'll do something, He does it. Nothing gets in His way. He doesn't change His mind.

And that means God is committed to you being blessed with peace. He doesn't want your inner landscape to be filled with anxiety, fear, and worries. His peace is something you can rely on. It won't go away. It won't change. It's there for the taking.

When anxiety overcomes me, Lord, remind me
that You have made a covenant of peace with me.
When worries multiply, teach me to turn to You.

JOY

When he arrived and saw this evidence of
God's blessing, he was filled with joy.

ACTS 11:23 NLT

One of the blessings God gives you is joy—and all His other blessings increase that joy. As God brings new people into your life, your joy increases. As He helps you with your work and your relationships, you feel happier. When He reveals to you the beauties of nature, your heart leaps up. When He blesses you with the fruit of the Spirit—love, peace, gentleness, self-control—your joy is magnified. Joy is like a spring of water that keeps spilling into your life.

Some days you may think the spring has run dry. You may feel as though you'll never be joyful again—but be patient. Joy will once more well up in your life. At first, it may just be a tiny trickle, but then it will grow into a rushing stream that fills your heart.

Thank You, God, for blessing me with joy.

A LAMP

Your word is a lamp to guide my feet and a light for my path.

PSALM 119:105 NLT

This verse promises that God's "word" will guide you. But what exactly is God's "word"? The Hebrew word that was used here refers to any sort of communication. So how does God communicate with you?

One way is through the Bible. Scripture can shed light into your heart and mind, helping you see God's direction for your life. God can also speak to you through other people, through the world of nature, and through your own thoughts (including your common sense). The best way God talks to you, though, is through Jesus, who is the Word. Jesus is God's communication to you in human form. As you study the life of Jesus in the Gospels, you will be blessed. And as you truly get to know Him, His light will be like a lamp, illumining the dark areas of your life.

Thank You, Jesus, for the light of Your life. Help me get to know You better. I want You to be my guide.

INSOMNIA

I will praise the Lord, who counsels me;
even at night my heart instructs me.
Psalm 16:7 NIV

Do you ever have nights when sleep won't come? Often, in those long, dark hours, life may seem bleaker than it looks in the light of day. Worries may loom larger. Your self-confidence might ebb to its all-time low. Problems can seem insurmountable.

But you can be blessed even in those sleepless nights. Whenever you have a bout of insomnia, you can use the extra time both to praise God and to listen to your own heart. If you surrender each worry, each sense of failure, each problem to God, He can use these nighttime moments to speak to you. He can calm the storms in your heart so that He can speak to you through your thoughts—and eventually, your dreams.

Thank You, God, that You are with me, both day and night. When I lie awake, remind me to turn my thoughts to You. Use the time to speak to me, I pray.

PERFECT LOVE

Such love has no fear, because perfect love expels all fear. If we are afraid, it is for fear of punishment.

1 JOHN 4:18 NLT

In this world, loving another person can be scary. Even the people who love you most will eventually, inevitably, let you down—just as you also will let them down. When you say or do the wrong thing, even accidentally, others may put up walls against you. They may retaliate with hurtful words and actions. You may be afraid that you will lose their love. Maybe you worry that the people you love will leave you.

But God's love is perfect. It will never let you down. He never pulls away from you, no matter what you do. His love is unconditional, His forgiveness absolute. You are blessed because you are totally secure in the love of God.

You know my fearful heart, God. Give me confidence in Your love.

THE BLESSING OF WORSHIP

"Worship the Lord *your God, and his blessing will be on your food and water. I will take away sickness from among you."*

Exodus 23:25 NIV

One way that God blesses you is through worship. The Hebrew word that has been translated as "worship" in this verse means "to serve" or "to work for," in the way that a farmer works his land or an employee works for her employer.

We can worship God in many ways. One way we can serve Him is by working to protect the planet that He created and gave to us as our home. As we do so, He has promised to bless our food and water. Human greed interferes with both the health of our souls and the health of the earth—but worship restores all life to the health God intended.

Thank You, God, for Your creation. Show me practical ways that I can work to protect it. I want to worship You in every way I can.

POWER AND WEALTH TO SERVE

If you start thinking to yourselves, "I did all this. And all by myself. I'm rich. It's all mine!"—well, think again. Remember that God, your God, gave you the strength to produce all this wealth.

Deuteronomy 8:17–18 msg

The words used in the original language to refer to "wealth" imply more than just monetary riches. They imply wealth that is tied together with strength. The meaning hints at a well-equipped army that has all the supplies it needs to be powerful. This is yet another way that you are blessed. God gives you everything you need to be a strong force for good in the world.

But even then, God wants you to remember where your resources came from. God longs to bless you with both strength and financial security. He wants you to have enough of everything you need to serve Him—but He also wants you to remember to give Him the credit.

God, I want to do good for You in the world. Give me what I need to be strong. Help me trust that You know exactly how much of each resource I truly need to be able to serve You.

THE BEAUTIFUL WORLD

Ever since the world was created, people have seen the earth and sky. Through everything God made, they can clearly see his invisible qualities—his eternal power and divine nature.

ROMANS 1:20 NLT

God has created a beautiful world for us to live in. The earth and the sky are filled to overflowing with amazing things—enormous trees and tiny fern fronds, flaming sunsets and star-strewn night skies, birdsong and whale song, summer thunderstorms and the one-of-a-kind intricacies of snowflakes. Each lovely thing reveals to us God's wonder and power. As we soak up nature's beauty, we draw close to God's heart.

You are blessed because you live in such a beautiful world!

Today, dear Lord, open my eyes to see the beauty of Your creation. May I not walk blindly through my day, so preoccupied with my own thoughts and worries that I overlook the wonderful world You have created. Thank You for blessing me with such loveliness.

JOYOUS STRENGTH

Strength and joy are in his dwelling place.

1 CHRONICLES 16:27 NIV

God's dwelling place is His home, and He has invited you to live there with Him. It's a place of great joy, but it's also a place where you can grow strong. Weakness and sadness often come together. When you feel as though you're too weak to accomplish anything, you may feel blue and depressed. Your self-concept suffers. You may start measuring yourself against others around you and find yourself lacking.

But it doesn't have to be that way. Stop focusing on your own flaws and shortcomings—and instead turn your eyes to God. He is welcoming you with open arms into His house—a place where joy and strength go hand in hand.

Thank You, God, that I can make my home with You. When I am weak, give me Your strength, and when I am sad, give me Your joy.

SKY, SEA, AND EARTH

"God, who helps you. . .who blesses you with blessings of the skies above, blessings of the deep springs below."

Genesis 49:25 niv

Our minds cannot grasp the full beauty, power, and meaning of God's nature. The Bible uses metaphors to help us understand. From the Old Testament through the New, scripture speaks of God as light and as water (as well as a host of other things). Each of these metaphors is like a handle designed to help us grab hold of God; using these word images helps us get a little closer to grasping just who God is.

So the next time you look up at a deep blue sky, remember that it is an expression of God's blessing. When you feel the sun on your face or moonlight streams through your window, think of God's light shining in your heart. And when you see water spilling clear and bright along a riverbed or tossing in the ocean's waves, remember that Jesus is a well of living water springing up within you. Sky and sea and earth, all give expression to our amazing Lord.

Thank You, Creator, for blessing me through the images of the natural world.

ETERNAL PATHS

Search me, God, and know my heart; put me to the test and know my anxious thoughts; and see if there is any hurtful way in me, and lead me in the everlasting way.

PSALM 139:23–24 NASB

God promises to bless you with His guidance throughout your life. But He guides gently, quietly, without fanfare or fuss. Often, when you ask for direction, you won't get any immediate answers. You need to be patient and take the time to be alone and quiet with the Lord. During these quiet times, you need to be honest—with God and with yourself—so that His Spirit can reveal to you any attitudes, thoughts, or behaviors that are destructive to you or others. If you open your heart and mind to God, He will lead you along paths that lead to eternal life.

God, I know You already know everything about me. You know me better than I know myself. Help me find time every day to be alone with You so that You can reveal my own heart and mind to me. Guide me, I pray.

PATIENT LOVE

Love is patient, love is kind. . .it keeps every confidence, it believes all things, hopes all things, endures all things.

1 CORINTHIANS 13:4, 7 NASB

You may think of these verses as being a description of how you should love others (which of course they are). But these familiar words also describe how God loves you. He is patient with you, no matter how many times you fall on your face, no matter how long you take to learn something, no matter how often you push Him away. He never stops believing in you. He always hopes for the best in your life. He's willing to put up with you for as long as it takes. You are blessed because God never stops loving you. He will never give up on you.

Thank You, God, for being patient with me.
Thank You for Your kindness.

SHOWERS OF BLESSING

"I'll make a covenant of peace with them. . . . I'll make them and everything around my hill a blessing. I'll send down plenty of rain in season—showers of blessing! The trees in the orchards will bear fruit, the ground will produce, they'll feel content and safe on their land, and they'll realize that I am God."

EZEKIEL 34:25–27 MSG

God wants to bless you spiritually (with love, peace, joy, patience, and many other spiritual qualities), but He also wants to bless you in the physical world. If you think of physical blessings, what comes to mind? Maybe a raise or a new car? Maybe things like good health or your dream house? God has nothing against those blessings, and when He promises to bless you, He means in every way possible.

However, God doesn't send good things into your life based on positive thinking or the law of attraction. Instead, when you let go of your self-centered wishes, when you surrender your entire life to God, He will shower you with all kinds of blessings—and they'll be exactly what you need.

Lord, I know You know what I need better than I do. Help me trust You to give me abundant blessings.

TREES

The Lord God made all sorts of trees grow up from the ground—
trees that were beautiful and that produced delicious fruit.

Genesis 2:9 NLT

At the beginning of the Bible, in the book of Genesis, we read the story of God's creation of the world. Even today, so many ages later, nature is God's masterpiece, an endlessly beautiful and varied expression of divine imagination. The many kinds of trees that we see growing, in forests and along city streets—pines and oaks, palms and willows, maples and tamarinds—are God's poems. They speak to us of God's unending power, creativity, and love.

So today when you see a tree, stop for a moment and really look at it. See it as a window into God's nature. Let it bless you.

Lord God, thank You for making trees and grass, flowers and vines.
Give me eyes to see Your beauty shining through the world.

COMMUNITY

"For where two or three gather in my name, there am I with them."

MATTHEW 18:20 NIV

God blesses us through other people. Although we all need time alone, we also need each other. Jesus and His followers taught that the church—which is actually a community built on relationships between people—is God's presence on earth. Together, we who follow Jesus are His body. Although He is no longer with us here in the flesh, together we are called to be His hands and arms, feet and legs. Together, we can bring hope and love to those who are poor in spirit and body.

Even if your "church" is only two or three friends praying together, supporting each other in the Lord's work, you are blessed—for Jesus is there with you.

Thank You, Jesus, for the people You have brought into my life. May we work together to be Your body.

JOY AND STRENGTH

"Don't be dejected and sad, for the joy of the Lord is your strength!"
NEHEMIAH 8:10 NLT

Have you ever had the impression that Christianity is a gloomy set of rules, that Christians go around with long faces? Unfortunately, there are Christians in the world who act like that. But that's not the sort of faith the Bible describes. The Bible speaks again and again of the Lord's joy.

Sadness can weaken your heart. It can rob you of hope and fill you with fear. But you have a relationship with the Creator of the universe, and He wants to share His eternal gladness with you. His joy will make you strong and brave, able to face the challenges of life. You are blessed with the joy of the Lord.

Joyful Lord, may others see in me Your strength,
Your kindness, and Your love.

WISDOM AND HEALING

The words of the wise bring healing.
PROVERBS 12:18 NLT

None of us know everything. No matter how educated we are or how mature, we all have times when our knowledge and experience run out. We face situations that leave us feeling confused and overwhelmed. We may even feel a little broken. In times like those, it's a good thing that we can rely on others' knowledge. Friends and teachers, counselors and pastors are just a few of the people who may be able to share their wisdom with us.

When you find yourself in a situation where you lack the knowledge you need, be humble enough to ask for help. Open your mind and heart to the wisdom and healing you need. When you do, you'll be blessed!

Thank You, Lord of love, for putting other people in my life, people who have skills and wisdom they can share with me.

GOD HAS YOUR BACK

Though a mighty army surrounds me, my heart will not be afraid. Even if I am attacked, I will remain confident.

PSALM 27:3 NLT

Sometimes circumstances seem to conspire against us, so that an entire army of problems surrounds us, all at the same time. And yet even then, the psalmist said we don't need to be afraid. We can remain calm, confident of God's love and care.

Confidence is one of the great blessings you can gain from the hard times you encounter. It may not be immediate, but with each problem you face, you will become sure of God's power to overcome even your life's steepest challenges. And the next time you face some hardship or trial, you'll remember what God did for you the last time. You'll be able to trust that just as He cared for you in the past, He will do so again. He is stronger than any enemy you will ever face!

Increase my confidence in You, Lord. When I feel surrounded, help me trust that You always have my back. You will defend me.

STORMS

Many waters cannot quench love, neither can the floods drown it.

SONG OF SOLOMON 8:7 KJV

God loves you endlessly, limitlessly, unconditionally—but that doesn't mean hard things won't come into your life. God's love won't magically protect you from all the world's storms of sorrow and pain. God does promise, however, to be with you in the storms. Even when the rain is pouring down and the floodwaters are rising all around you, you are blessed because His love will never fail you. Nothing that enters your life, no matter how difficult or painful, can drown the love God has for you. And when the storms are over, you may be surprised to find that they bring forth new life, something unexpected and wonderful you never dreamed could come into existence.

When hard times come, Lord, remind me that Your love still surrounds me. I can count on You to keep me safe.

YOUR HOME

My people shall dwell in a peaceable habitation,
and in sure dwellings, and in quiet resting places.

ISAIAH 32:18 KJV

In this verse, God is promising to bless your home—and He's not talking about a vague, hard-to-grasp spiritual blessing. Instead, He's promising you something concrete: a home where you can feel safe, where you can rest and be quiet at the end of a long day.

So the next time you look around your house and see worn carpets, clutter, or smudgy windows, remember that your home is blessed by God—and He lives there with you!

Thank You, Lord, that I am Yours, and You have blessed me in so many ways. I am grateful for my home. Please bless its every corner. Make Your home here too, with me.

YOUR JOB

Do your best. Work from the heart for your real Master, for God, confident that you'll get paid in full when you come into your inheritance.

COLOSSIANS 3:23–24 MSG

When the apostle Paul wrote this passage of scripture, he understood how frustrating it can be to work hard and get paid too little—or to feel as though your employer doesn't appreciate your full skill and effort. "Don't worry about any of that," he was saying here. "You're really working for Jesus. And one day, in eternity, He'll see you get paid exactly what you deserve."

No matter what your job or profession is, your real boss is Jesus. So even on those days when you hate your job—and we all have at least a few of those days—Jesus will bless your work.

Jesus, may I see You in my daily work—and may I work to please You. Thank You for my job. May it be an opportunity for me to serve You.

FRIENDS AND FAMILY

A friend loves at all times, and a brother is born for adversity.

PROVERBS 17:17 NASB

When things are going your way, you may be tempted to think that you don't need anyone's help. You feel strong and self-confident. You may think that you're so spiritually mature that you can go it alone, just you and the Lord. That's a pretty great way to feel.

But sooner or later, all of us face times when everything seems to fall apart. We can't cope with life so smoothly anymore; even our faith may falter. We feel as though we're drowning.

If you've found yourself in a situation like that and a friend offered you her hand, pulling you back onto dry land, then you know how blessed you are. God created friends and families so that we can help each other get through life's hard times.

I'm so grateful, Lord, for the people who love me.
Thank You for all the ways they make my life easier.
May I bless them as they have blessed me.

LAUGHTER

You make known to me the path of life; you will fill me with joy in your presence, with eternal pleasures at your right hand.

Psalm 16:11 NIV

The Hebrew word that is translated "joy" in this verse is *samach*, which means, literally, "mirth." This is the sort of joy that makes you laugh out loud. It gives you the giggles. Your face breaks into a smile, and you laugh easily.

Laughter is part of God's perfect plan for human beings, and a sense of humor is one of His blessings. Scientific research has found that laughter is medically good for us. It decreases stress and helps protect us against stress-related diseases. Our faith is not meant to be a gloomy, stern thing, filled with disapproval and constant *nos*. Instead, those of us who follow Jesus say "yes!" to life. We enjoy life! We smile and laugh a lot. And our joy isn't fleeting. It will last for eternity.

Thank You, God, for showing me the path of life—
a path of joy and laughter and eternal pleasure.

WORKING FOR THE KINGDOM

And the work of righteousness will be peace, and the service of righteousness, quietness and confidence forever.

ISAIAH 32:17 NASB

What if every day when you started your work, you remembered that you were serving God and His kingdom? What if instead of obsessing over successes and failures, over paychecks and promotions, you focused all your heart, mind, and body on building the kingdom of God?

If you do that, this verse promises that you'll be blessed with peace. You'll have a quiet confidence that you are doing the work God needs you to be doing. You are not just doing a job. You are working for eternity.

May the work I do please You, Lord. Keep my perspective aligned with Yours so that I see things from the point of view of Your kingdom. Show me ways that I can make a difference in the lives of the people I meet at work.

IN GOD'S ARMS

Praise the Lord; praise God our savior!
For each day he carries us in his arms.

PSALM 68:19 NLT

When we count our blessings, we usually make a list of the good things in our lives, things like warm houses, good health, plenty of food, friends and family. Sometimes we may remember to include spiritual and emotional blessings—peace, joy, hope, and love. But often we overlook the greatest blessing of all—the presence of the Lord.

God, the Creator of the universe, is present with you every moment of your day. He is carrying you in His arms. There is no greater blessing than that!

I praise You, Lord, my Savior. Thank You for loving me so much. I am so glad that You are always with me. When I forget You, remind me that You are with me, carrying me in Your arms.

THE SHELTER OF GOD'S PRESENCE

In the shelter of your presence. . .you keep them safe. . .from accusing tongues.

PSALM 31:20 NIV

Do you ever worry about what people think of you? To one extent or another, most of us do. We want people to like us. We want them to approve of the way we look and act and talk. If we're honest with ourselves, we probably have to admit that we want to impress other people so that they think well of us. When we succeed, we feel good about ourselves, but when we don't—when people criticize us or just give us a dirty look—we often feel less worthy, full of shame and self-doubt.

But you don't have to live like that, captive to the opinions of others. Instead, you can live in the shelter of God's presence. You'll be safe there from the negative opinions of others because you'll be surrounded by God's love. If God approves of you, who cares what others think? You have been blessed with the love and approval of God Himself.

When people hurt my feelings, Lord, remind me to run into Your arms.

HAPPINESS

Blessed is the one You choose and allow to approach You.

PSALM 65:4 NASB

The Hebrew word that is translated as "blessed" in this verse means simply "happy." You are blessed because God chose you—and He longs to make you happy. When you draw near to Him, your heart will fill with joy. Of course you'll still have the ups and downs that everyone else has. Sorrows will come, and you'll face days that challenge you. But through it all, God is seeking to make you happy. He is a God of joy, and He wants to share His joy with you.

Thank You, God, for the joy You give me.
Encourage my heart when I am sad, and remind me that I will again know the happiness You have planned for me.

GOD'S RESTFUL PRESENCE

"My Presence will go with you, and I will give you rest."

EXODUS 33:14 NIV

Sometimes life just seems so hard! You face one challenge after another—sickness, problems with your parents or children, financial worries, car troubles, broken relationships. . . Do you ever find yourself saying, "If only life would get back to normal"? But it never does, does it?

Have you considered that life's endless challenges may be what normal life looks like? When you do accept that fact, you can look for rest and relief from another source—from the one who loves you unconditionally and blesses you infinitely. When you turn to God, you'll find His presence already there waiting for you. He will bless you with rest even in the midst of life's trials and frustrations.

Give me Your rest, Lord. I need it so desperately.

PRESENT TENSE

The LORD bestows his blessing, even life forevermore.

PSALM 133:3 NIV

Do you ever think about eternity? Most of us have a vague idea about it as an unknown realm far off in the future. In this verse, however, the psalmist didn't use the future tense; he wrote in the present. His words imply that the blessing of eternal life starts right now, in this very moment.

The Hebrew word that is translated "life" in this verse has a breadth of meaning. It means "to come to life in a new way," "to be restored to life after being dead," "to be healed or to recover from an illness," and "to be nourished." All those blessings are contained in this verse. And they're all yours *right now*. You don't have to wait until you die.

Thank You, Lord of life, that You bring me to life in new ways; that You heal me, inside and out; that You nourish me; and that You give me victory over death.

WHEN YOU CAN'T FEEL GOD'S PRESENCE

O Lord, why do you stand so far away?
Why do you hide when I am in trouble?

Psalm 10:1 NLT

Do you ever find yourself saying words like the psalmist's to God? If we're honest, probably most of us have. Even Jesus, when He was hanging on the cross, cried out, "My God, why have You forsaken Me?"

No matter how many Bible verses we read about God blessing us in the midst of trials and troubles, it's hard to *feel* blessed when life is full of pain and anxiety. And just as the psalmist and Jesus expressed these feelings, it's okay to tell God how we feel. We don't need to feel guilty for wondering if God is really still there, if He really still loves us, when everything around us seems to say otherwise. Sometimes, all we have to offer God is bitterness, discouragement, and anger.

You can be honest with God—and when you are, He can bless even your pain and anxiety. Even if you can't feel His presence with you, He is still there.

Thank You, Lord, that You never abandon me.
Thank You that You are there even when I can't feel You.

WELCOME

Gladness and joy will overtake them,
and sorrow and sighing will flee away.
ISAIAH 35:10 NIV

The Bible is filled with references to joy. If we look at the original languages, whether Hebrew or Greek, we find various shades of meaning. In this verse, the Hebrew word translated as "gladness and joy" means exactly that—but it has an added ingredient, for the word also means "welcome."

This is a joy that runs after you with open arms. It longs to bring you home. Even if you are deep in depression, wandering down dark and dreary paths, it catches up with you sooner or later. It chases away all your sadness, and it leads you back to the place where you can be whole and healthy and happy. "Come home," God says through this word. "Come home and be blessed."

Lord, chase away my sadness with Your joy. Take me home to You.

HIDING PLACES

You are my hiding place; You keep me from trouble;
You surround me with songs of deliverance.

PSALM 32:7 NASB

If your heart is full of doubt and despair, can you still experience God's blessings? Yes. God is not limited by your emotions.

Sometimes, though, we have to endure our negative emotions for a while. Sooner or later, the bad feelings will lift, and we will once more see the light. But in the meantime, we just have to keep putting one foot in front of the other.

During this time, God will give you hiding places where you can find respite from your troubles. These secret places of safety come in many forms—prayer, scripture, nature, books, music, and the support of friends and family, to name just a few. Each one of these is a place where you can escape, if only temporarily, and experience God's presence.

Lord, I need to hear Your songs of deliverance.
Please lift my spirits so I can once more experience Your joy.

A MOTHER'S COMFORT

"As a mother comforts her child, so will I comfort you."

ISAIAH 66:13 NIV

Even if you aren't a mother yourself, you probably either had a loving mother or know someone who demonstrated a mother's love to you. Human mothers teach us about God's love. They demonstrate the kind of love that doesn't hesitate but always rushes to help and comfort. If their children are in danger, most mothers will do whatever they have to in order to save them. In good times and in bad, they are focused on their children's well-being.

And you are blessed because that is exactly the way God loves you! When you are sad or troubled, you can run to Him—and He will comfort you the way a mother comforts her child.

God, thank You for Your comforting love.

CHILDREN

"All your children will be taught by the LORD,
and great will be their peace."

ISAIAH 54:13 NIV

Even if you don't have your own children, there are probably children in your life whom you love. But as much as you love them—and you really do!—you'd probably have to admit that at one time or another you let them down. After all, you're only human, and human beings make mistakes.

So it's good to know that God will fill in the gaps that we leave in our children's education. As this verse promises, God Himself will teach our children! As we surrender our children—and our mistakes—to God, He will bless us all with His peace.

Thank You for the children in my life, Lord. I thank You for all the ways that they bless my life—and I ask now that You would bless them in return. Teach them what they need to know in order to grow into strong, loving, healthy adults.

YOUR NAME ON GOD'S LIPS

"Come, you who are blessed by my Father, inherit the Kingdom prepared for you from the creation of the world."

MATTHEW 25:34 NLT

In this verse, the Greek word translated "blessed" means "to speak well of, to say words that give or create something good." Speaking is important in the Bible, and words have power (this is why we are cautioned to use our words carefully). In Genesis, God spoke the world into being. And your name is on God's lips. You were in His mind before the creation of the world, and He spoke your very being into existence. You are blessed because you are a child of the kingdom—and God calls you by name!

Thank You, Father, that You bless me in so many ways. I am so grateful that through Your Spirit, I can inherit Your kingdom.

THE HELPER

"I will ask the Father, and He will give you another Helper, so that He may be with you forever."

JOHN 14:16 NASB

The disciples had the amazing privilege of living side by side with Jesus in His physical form. They walked with Him through the hills of Galilee, and they talked with Him. They shared their lives with Him, laughed with Him, and got to know Him intimately. They knew His voice and the shape of His hands; they saw His smile and looked into His eyes.

But then Jesus' friends faced the terrible loss of His presence. How much that must have hurt them! But Jesus understood how they were going to feel, and He promised them that even though they would no longer be able to see and touch Him, He would send His Spirit to be with them instead. How blessed they were!

And how blessed you are—for the Spirit is with you as well, within you, helping you, walking with you.

Thank You, Jesus, for sending Your Spirit to help me with my life. May I learn to follow His guidance.

THE VALLEY OF WEEPING

When they walk through the Valley of Weeping, it will become a place of refreshing springs. The autumn rains will clothe it with blessings.

Psalm 84:6 NLT

All lives contain times of weeping. Trouble comes in many forms. . .and sooner or later, it does always come. When it does, our hearts break within us. We would do anything to avoid this sorrow.

But even when you find yourself in a dark valley, God promises to bless you. As you stumble through the darkness, you will find springs of new life hidden there in that rocky land. The tears on your face will turn to blessing. God will walk with you. He will not abandon you.

Lord, thank You that even when my heart is breaking, You have promised to bless me. I don't understand how that can be possible—but I know You always keep Your word. Help me trust You even during my times of weeping.

DEATH'S SHADOW

"The people living in darkness have seen a great light; on those living in the land of the shadow of death a light has dawned."

MATTHEW 4:16 NIV

We live in a culture that tries to avoid death's reality. We often act as though we can put it off forever. We believe that there is something "unnatural" about it, instead of accepting that death is a part of life. Every person who is born will one day die.

And yet, death has always been the great mystery, the dark unknown that overshadows all of life's light. For us, death means sorrow. It means being forced to say goodbye to the people we love. For some of us, the word may bring fear, even terror.

In this verse, however, Jesus tells you that you don't have to be afraid of death. It is not the end. Night may fall—but a new dawn will come.

Thank You, Jesus, for Your promise of everlasting life.
I want to live so close to You that I lose my fear of death.

SPIRITUAL GIFTS

I long to see you so that I may impart to you
some spiritual gift to make you strong.
ROMANS 1:11 NIV

When Paul wrote these words, he was referring to a particular kind of blessing—a spiritual gift that would give strength and confidence. The Greek word used here is *charisma*, a gift of grace that empowers the recipient to work on behalf of God's kingdom.

Gifts of this nature are given freely. You don't have to do anything to earn them except give yourself to God so He can use you. You won't be able to see a spiritual gift—but you will be blessed by its power. It will fill your life with love, joy, and peace. It will give you spiritual strength so that God can use you more effectively.

I want to be of use to You, Lord, and so I ask that You give me whatever spiritual gifts I need to serve You. May I carry Your love out into the world.

A CONSTANT STREAM

God's love has been poured out into our hearts through the Holy Spirit.

ROMANS 5:5 NIV

God's love touches your entire life. When you learn to look for His love, you can see evidence of it everywhere you turn—in the beauty of nature, in the warmth of friendship, in the tenderness of human love. Even better, He pours His love directly into your heart. You can be like a cup that God never stops filling. Love is a constant stream flowing into you from God, and eventually that love runs over. Because you have been blessed with God's infinite love, you can pass that blessing on to others. You are doubly blessed!

God, I am so grateful for all the ways You give me Your love.
Show me how to pass Your love on to everyone I see today.

LAUGHTER AND SONG

When the righteous see God in action they'll laugh,
they'll sing, they'll laugh and sing for joy.

PSALM 68:3 MSG

If you ever thought that the Bible was a gloomy book filled with don'ts and harsh rules, then verses like this one, filled with song and laughter, should convince you that your heavenly Father is actually a joyful God. The Hebrew word that has been translated as "joy" carries the meaning of rejoicing in triumph.

God wants to make you so happy that you laugh out loud. He wants you to exult. You are blessed because the Creator of the universe is working on your behalf. He is involved in all the details of your life in a personal, intimate, ongoing way. And He wants you to sing with joy when you see Him triumph over everything that would hold you back from His perfect will for your life.

Thank You, God of song and laughter, for all that You are doing in my life. I'm so glad I have the privilege to watch You in action.

SURRENDER

"And everyone who has left houses or brothers or sisters or father or mother or children or farms on account of My name, will receive many times as much, and will inherit eternal life."

MATTHEW 19:29 NASB

God calls us to live in loving relationship with each other—and yet when Jesus spoke the words of this verse, we might think He was saying the exact opposite. In fact, it sounds as though He's asking us to abandon our children and our parents, our work and our homes. It's hard to read these words.

But what Jesus is really asking for is the absolute surrender of everything we love. Nothing can be more important to us than He is, not even the people whom we love most. He's saying to us, "Let go of your control. Give everything to Me."

If you can hear and obey this message, you will be blessed not only with eternal life but also with earthly blessings. Surrender everything to God—and He will give everything back to you!

God, help me trust You with my entire life.

SIN—OR LIFE?

Those who live only to satisfy their own sinful nature will harvest decay and death from that sinful nature. But those who live to please the Spirit will harvest everlasting life from the Spirit.

GALATIANS 6:8 NLT

We have built our idea of "sin" into something very large and dirty—but the Greek meaning of this word is quite simple. It means "failing to hit the mark." In other words, when we let our selfishness run the show, we are like arrows that miss their targets. Our target is life, but unless we surrender ourselves to the Spirit, our arrows are hitting death instead of life. It's as simple as that.

You have a choice. You don't have to keep shooting your arrows in the wrong direction. When you choose instead to aim toward God, your life will be changed in the here and now. Your life will be made whole, all its broken places mended. And you will be blessed with new life, a life that will never end.

Spirit, I want Your life. Remove from me, I pray, all that is pointed toward death. Make me into a person who exudes life with everything I do.

UNFAILING LOVE

*"I have loved you, my people, with an everlasting love.
With unfailing love I have drawn you to myself."*

JEREMIAH 31:3 NLT

God's love is everlasting. In other words, it never ends. It has no limits. It is broader and deeper than anything you can comprehend, because there are no boundary lines it refuses to cross. And you don't have to earn it, because it is unconditional.

Wherever you go, God's love follows you. It pulls at your heart, drawing you ever closer to God. Somewhere, inside you, you know God's love is the source of all your joy. God's everlasting, unfailing love isn't just an aspect of eternity; it *is* eternity. You are blessed because God's love lasts forever.

Thank You, God, for Your love that never fails.
I am so grateful that You call me Your beloved.

ABUNDANCE

God is able to bless you abundantly.

2 CORINTHIANS 9:8 NIV

When Paul wrote this sentence to the church at Corinth, he was talking about God's power, something that is over and above anything else we've ever encountered. God uses that power to give grace and kindness to us that is also over and above anything we can even imagine. God's power is immeasurable, and His blessings are abundant. Each day brings new blessings. Each stage of your life will reveal new ways that God's grace can touch your life. You're not just blessed a little bit; you are blessed abundantly, immensely, beyond your wildest dreams!

Teach me, Lord, to see Your blessings in my life.
Thank You for Your grace and kindness.

ANGELS

The angel of His presence saved them.

ISAIAH 63:9 NASB

Whether or not you can sense God's presence, He is always with you. He understands, though, that human perceptions are limited; He knows that we often feel bereft and alone. That's why He sometimes sends "angels" into our lives, people or creatures we can touch with our hands and see and hear with our physical eyes and ears.

The Hebrew word that's been translated as "angel" in this verse means a "messenger, ambassador, or envoy." In other words, someone whom God sends to carry His messages to you. If you think about it, you'll probably realize that you've been blessed with many angels in your life—people who make real to you the presence of God. Even a dog or cat that expresses unconditional love can be God's angel, carrying the message of divine love. All you need to do is listen.

Thank You, Lord of love, for sending angels into my life.
I am so grateful for the messages of love You send my way.

GOD IS LOVE

God is love, and all who live in love live in God, and God lives in them.

1 JOHN 4:16 NLT

As Christians, sometimes we make our lives far more complicated than God ever intended them to be. Maybe we focus on theology, which is all fine and good in its place, but it can distract us from the love that God says is at the center of His will for our lives. Or some of us may worry a lot about dos and don'ts. We may think that our church is the only one that has got Christianity exactly "right," and we suspect that those people worshipping in the church across town have got it all "wrong." But the Bible says we should worry less about those things and instead focus on love.

Verses like this one make it very clear and simple: When you live in love, you are living in God, and God is living in you. You are blessed—and God uses you to bless others.

Teach me, God, to love as You love. May love be at the center of everything I do and say.

FOR GOD SO LOVED

"This is how much God loved the world: He gave his Son, his one and only Son. And this is why: so that no one need be destroyed; by believing in him, anyone can have a whole and lasting life. God didn't go to all the trouble of sending his Son merely to point an accusing finger, telling the world how bad it was. He came to help, to put the world right again."

JOHN 3:16–17 MSG

When we talk about God's love, it's not just a pretty phrase or a lofty theological concept. We see God's love in the person of Jesus, the full expression of the Father. Jesus came so that we would truly understand that we are loved.

God's love isn't generic. You are blessed because He loves one-of-a-kind *you*—and you can know God's love personally. The more you open yourself to His love, the more you will experience it and the more you will be able to trust Him. You can lean your entire life on God's love, knowing that He will never jerk it out from under you. How could He, when His very nature is love?

Thank You, Jesus, for bringing the Father's love to the world.

A VICTORY SONG

When the righteous see God in action they'll laugh, they'll sing, they'll laugh and sing for joy.

PSALM 68:3 MSG

The Hebrew word that's been translated as "joy" here is *alats*, meaning "exults, rejoices in triumph." It's the joy that the winning team feels at the end of the game. It's the kind of happiness that sings a victory song.

God is taking action in your life. His Spirit is moving and acting in amazing ways. You are blessed because the Creator of the world is working on your behalf, in a personal, intimate, ongoing way! As you see Him triumph over the forces of darkness, He will fill your heart with a victory song of joy.

I ask You, God, to show me the ways You are at work in my life. When I feel discouraged, help me see that You are still victorious.

THE DESIRES OF YOUR HEART

Take delight in the Lord, and he will give you the desires of your heart.

Psalm 37:4 NIV

Do you ever feel as though you have an empty place inside you, a hole that can never be filled, no matter how many things you get? You may try to fill that hole with all sorts of things—with money or prestige, with clothes or food, with popularity or power, with education or shopping sprees—and yet it never seems to go away.

There is nothing inherently wrong with any of those things, but they can never fill that emptiness inside us all. Nothing from this world can ever meet our deepest needs. Only God can do that. The Bible says that God put eternity into our hearts (Ecclesiastes 3:11). Deep inside our innermost beings, we yearn for all that eternity holds—all its abundance, wholeness, and beauty. This is what our hearts really crave—and only God can give us what they desire.

Be assured—when you delight in the Lord, He will never disappoint you. You will be blessed in ways that fill that empty hole inside.

Lord, teach me to seek my desires in You.

ALL YOU WANT IN LIFE

"You are my place of refuge. You are all I really want in life."

PSALM 142:5 NLT

God offers us a refuge in times of trouble, and blessings can come to you even in the midst of pain and challenge. In this verse, the psalmist's words remind you that in both good times and bad, God Himself is your safe place, that perfect spot where you feel completely and totally secure.

When you reach the place where God is the only thing you truly want (because everything else in life is wrapped up within His arms), then you'll no longer have to worry about loss and defeat, hardship and anxieties. Even death will no longer have the power to disturb your peace of mind. You can rest in the knowledge that you are blessed with the presence of the Lord.

Thank You, Lord of heaven and earth, that I can run to You whenever I feel insecure or anxious. Teach me that everything I want is truly hidden within Your perfect will for my life.

CALLING

The Lord is near to all who call on Him.

Psalm 145:18 NASB

The Hebrew word that's been translated as "call" in this verse doesn't mean that we're calling God the way we might call a dog, nor does it have the same meaning as calling a friend on the phone. No, the word used here is much stronger than either of those meanings that may come to mind when we first read the word *call*. It means to scream God's name so loud that everyone around us can hear. That kind of call is an affirmation of our faith in God.

You are blessed because God's presence is always with you. But you may not always feel that God is there. When you call out His name, though, that changes your own perceptions. You can finally *know* that the presence of the Lord is close to you. So don't be afraid to scream His name!

Lord, thank You that I can shout Your name when times get hard. I'm so glad that You are always listening for my call and that You will never leave me to manage my life without You.

PROSPEROUS

Beloved, I pray that in all respects you may prosper and be in good health, just as your soul prospers.

3 John 2 NASB

God wants you to do well in life. That's why He sends both physical and spiritual blessings into your life. He wants every bit of you to be healthy and prosperous—emotionally, physically, financially, spiritually, intellectually, socially. We tend to divide the spiritual world from the physical one, as though they were two separate things; but in this verse, John described a perspective where each sort of blessing flows into all the others. As you are spiritually blessed, your entire life—body, mind, and soul—will be blessed as well.

I'm so glad, Lord, that You bless my entire life.

YOUR WORK

God will lavish you with good things. . . . God will throw open the doors of his sky vaults and pour rain on your land on schedule and bless the work you take in hand.

DEUTERONOMY 28:11–12 MSG

In one way or another, you probably go to work almost every day. Whether you work at home or in an office, in a factory or in a classroom, in your yard or on a roadway, God promises to bless your work. Maybe you love your job, and you're excited about going to work. Or maybe you hate it, and you do it only for the paycheck. Either way, God has promised to throw open His "vaults," the places where He stores His resources, and rain down blessing on your work. Everything you do matters to Him—including your work—and He wants to lavish you with good things.

Thank You, generous Lord, for all You give to me. I ask Your blessing on my work. May the job I do be pleasing to You. Show me ways to serve You, even as I do my work.

NATURAL CONSEQUENCES

All these blessings will come on you and accompany you if you obey the LORD your God.

DEUTERONOMY 28:2 NIV

God always seeks to bless you. Some of His blessings—like the sun on our heads or the wind in the trees, the laughter of children or the love of a friend—are passed out lavishly, for absolutely everyone to enjoy. Sometimes God would bless us in other ways if He could, but our own decisions put us in places where His blessings can't reach us. It's not that God is punishing us for our disobedience, but there *are* natural consequences. When we choose to disregard God's guidance, we may find ourselves on paths that lead to destruction and pain.

But if you obey the Spirit's guiding within you, you'll be blessed with the fullness of God's gifts of life and love.

Give me an obedient heart, Spirit. May I listen for Your voice—and follow Your guidance.

LEAP FOR JOY

"What blessings await you when people hate you and exclude you and mock you and curse you as evil because you follow the Son of Man. When that happens, be happy! Yes, leap for joy!"

LUKE 6:22–23 NLT

These words of Jesus' don't seem to make much sense by earthly standards. Why would we be happy when people are mean to us? The Greek word Jesus used is *skirtaō*, which means "leap for joy," but it's also the same word used when a baby "quickens," when the mother first feels the movement of life.

So Jesus is saying that when you follow Him and feel misunderstood and separated from everyone around you, that's the very moment that something new will come to life inside you. You will begin to grow in new ways. You will be blessed as you experience a new kind of joy, a joy that's lively and exuberant.

Jesus, sometimes I have a hard time understanding Your words. I want to follow You though, no matter what—and I'll trust You to keep Your promises.

PRIORITIES

Those who seek the LORD lack no good thing.

PSALM 34:10 NIV

You are blessed by God in so many ways—but in this verse, the psalmist's words remind you to keep your priorities lined up with God's will. You don't need to worry about whether God is blessing you. You don't need to ask, "When?" or "How?" Instead, you need to turn your attention to God. Focus on Him. And when you do, He will take care of your needs, both the material ones and the spiritual. He will make sure you don't lack anything. When you make God your priority, you can trust Him to take care of everything else.

Thank You, Lord, for the many, many promises You have given me in Your Word. Help me let Your promises take root in my heart so that I can trust You more and more. Show me if anything has come between me and You. I want You to have first place in my life.

UNFOLDING GRACE

Not a day goes by without his unfolding grace.

2 CORINTHIANS 4:16 MSG

Imagine a cloth that's been tightly folded into a tiny square only a few inches across. At first glance, this cloth seems pretty insignificant. Now picture yourself unfolding that square of cloth—and discovering that it's not small at all. The more you unfold it, the longer and wider it becomes. Instead of being something so small that it could easily be overlooked, this cloth is longer and wider than anything you ever imagined.

God's blessings are like that. Not a day goes by that He's not unfolding new expressions of His grace in your life. His cloth of blessing is endless!

When my life seems barren and dry, Lord, remind me that You are still unfolding new blessings. Teach me to wait for You and to be content with Your timing.

BELOVED

"The Lord bless you and keep you; the Lord make His face shine upon you, and be gracious to you; the Lord lift up His countenance upon you, and give you peace."

Numbers 6:24–26 NKJV

Rest in the knowledge that you are truly blessed. You are the Lord's beloved—and He will protect you, shine His light on you, and give you peace. Each moment of your life, His grace is flowing out to you. You make Him smile.

Oh Lord, I cannot comprehend all the ways You have blessed me. Thank You that I not only have my entire lifetime to experience Your goodness, but I also have all of eternity. I am so grateful to be Your beloved child.

SCRIPTURE INDEX

OLD TESTAMENT

Genesis

1:22 5
2:9 141
17:20 112
41:16 73
49:25 137

Exodus

23:25 133
33:14 155

Numbers

6:24–26 186
25:12 128

Deuteronomy

7:9 89
8:17–18 134
28:1–2 20
28:2 182
28:3–5 27
28:6 39
28:8 33
28:11–12 181
30:16 77

Judges

18:6 114

1 Samuel

16:7 102

1 Chronicles

16:27 136

2 Chronicles

15:7 69

Nehemiah

8:10 143

Psalms

1:1–3 81
5:3 78
9:9 123
10:1 157
10:17 72
16:7 131
16:11 150
23:1–3 41
23:4 47
23:5 .... 51, 124
27:3 145
31:20 153
32:7 159
32:8 116
34:10 184
36:5 80
37:4 177
37:5 48
52:8 118
65:4 154
68:3 .... 168, 176
68:19 152
73:26 104
78:24 75

81:10 37
84:5 53
84:6 164
84:11 23
92:12–14 56
98:4 115
104:24 127
105:4 71
115:14 46
119:105 .... 108, 130
133:3 .... 84, 156
136:23–26 76
139:23–24 138
142:5 178
145:18 179
147:13 31

Proverbs

3:27 49
10:22 29
12:18 144
13:4 68
13:12 98
14:21 34
16:3 99
16:9 67
17:17 149

Ecclesiastes

4:6 52
7:14 83

Song of Solomon

8:7 146

Isaiah

30:15 50
30:19–22 40
30:21 117
32:15–18 113
32:17 151
32:18 147
35:10 158
40:31 18
41:10 9
48:17 121
50:7 111
54:13 161
63:9 173
66:13 160

Jeremiah

17:7–8 25
29:11 24
31:3 171

Ezekiel

34:25–27 140

Hosea

14:5–6 66

Joel

2:23 95
2:26 43

Malachi
3:10 15
4:2 54

NEW TESTAMENT

Matthew
4:16 .... 119, 165
5:3 58
5:4 59
5:5 60
5:6 61
5:7 62
5:8 63
5:9 64
5:11–12 65
6:8 26
6:25–27 21
6:28–30 14
6:32–33 28
11:28–30 109
18:20 142
19:29 169
25:34 162

Mark
5:34 120

Luke
6:22–23 183
6:38 8
12:32 93

John
1:16–17 11
3:16–17 175
7:37–39 107
10:27–28 74
14:16 163
14:27 86
15:9 122
15:13 85
16:33 55

Acts
11:23 129

Romans
1:11 166
1:20 135
5:3–5 126
5:5 167
8:6 13
8:35, 37–39 88
12:6 94
15:4 45

1 Corinthians
2:9 36
13:4, 7 139
15:58 100
16:13–14 79

2 Corinthians
1:20–22 105

4:16 185
5:17 32
7:10 90
9:6–7 17
9:8 172
9:10–12 22
10:5 13

Galatians

3:13–14 5
6:2 110
6:8 170

Ephesians

1:3 12
1:3–6 97
3:20 16
4:22–24 106
6:10–13 103

Philippians

1:6 38
4:19 10

Colossians

2:6–7 57
3:23–24 148

1 Thessalonians

5:17 26

Hebrews

10:23 70
12:1–2 30

James

1:5 35
1:12 19
1:17 7

1 Peter

1:2 96
3:3–5 101
3:9 42
5:7 92

2 Peter

1:3–4 44

1 John

1:6–7 91
3:1 87
4:9 125
4:16 174
4:18 132

3 John

2 180

Jude

24 82